Ron Bowman

WHEN
YOU
BUILD
YOUR
CHURCH

WHEN YOU BUILD YOUR CHURCH

SECOND EDITION

by John R. Scotford

CHANNEL PRESS, INC.   GREAT NECK, N. Y.

Library of Congress Catalog Card Number: 58-8051

Chapter

Illustrations

Bethel Lutheran Church, Minneapolis, Minnesota

University Lutheran Church, Cambridge, Massachusetts

First Free Methodist Church, Seattle, Washington

First Methodist Church, Midland, Michigan

First Presbyterian Church, Birmingham, Michigan

Clifton Lutheran Church, Marblehead, Massachusetts

The Church in Silver Lake, Cuyahoga Falls, Ohio

First Methodist Church, Niles, Ohio

Westminster Presbyterian Church, Austin, Minnesota

Holy Trinity Episcopal Church, Oxford, Ohio

Zion Evangelical and Reformed Church, Mount Clemens, Michigan

Westminster Presbyterian Church, Austin, Minnesota

University Lutheran Church, Cambridge, Massachusetts

Zion Evangelical and Reformed Church, Mount Clemens, Michigan

First Methodist Church, Midland, Michigan

Clifton Lutheran Church, Marblehead, Massachusetts

First Congregational Church, Austin, Minnesota

Chapel, Wittenberg College, Springfield, Ohio

WHEN

YOU

BUILD

YOUR

CHURCH

Chapter **1**

TO BUILD OR NOT TO BUILD

SHOULD we build? Most Protestant churches today must face this question; some six or seven thousand congregations each year for the next ten years will wrestle with the problem. For many churches the one really good answer will be a new building on a new site. For others the solution may be expansion and modernization of the structures they now have. Only a very few will find that the facilities they have inherited from yesterday are adequate for the needs of tomorrow.

Whatever its own answer may be, any congregation will move into the future more intelligently and more successfully if it gives serious thought to the conditions which are creating the present utterly unprecedented boom in church building.

The American people are spending upward of $800,000,000 a year on new religious buildings for three fundamental reasons: the birth rate, the motorcar, and the obsolescence of our existing churches. These conditions promise to continue. There is no reason to believe that babies are likely to lose their present popularity, or that the American people will cease to get around on rubber tires, or that old churches will suddenly become suited to new uses. A period of financial adversity might dam the flood for a time, but it cannot dry up the springs from which it flows. The question, "Should our church build?" may be postponed, but not escaped.

Behind the building boom lies the baby boom. Today's children are crowding the walls of our churches. In a very few years the "war babies" will begin to reproduce, and the tide of population will rise to new heights. The most basic reason for building new churches is that there are more people than ever before to use them.

The rising generation calls for more than the multiplication of walls and the expansion of roofs. The need is not merely for more space, but for different kinds of space. The age at which children now start to church is dropping: you have certainly seen six-weeks-old babies happily snoozing in ecclesiastical crib rooms, or have heard of three-weeks-old infants being carried to the House of God.

Our notions of how religious nurture should be administered to children have changed radically. Older folk can remember how they were seated on little red chairs in the more dismal portion of the church basement, while some well-meaning soul exhorted them simply "to be good." Contemporary young parents are living close to their children: they are keenly sensitive to the likes and dislikes of these young ones; they are aware of everything which affects the well-being of their offspring. The immediate instigation for one spacious educational building was the refusal of a prominent family to send their small children "up those rickety stairs to the little hole of a room" where the kindergarten met in what had once been a second-rate parsonage. Not only do we have more children than ever before, but the conscience of the church demands that each child have much more room today than in the past.

Except in our largest cities, rubber tires have taken the place of shoes in getting people from one place to another. By and large the smaller the community, the less do its residents walk. Farmers have been known to drive from the house to the barn! This change in our means of locomotion is affecting the church in many ways.

It has brought an increasing dispersal of our population. The distance between where people live and where they work and play is stretched farther with each passing year. Easy mobility is giving us a rash of new communities, and they in turn call for new churches. But the motorcar is also doing something much more subtle and possibly more disturbing. Quick and easy transportation has extended the range of choice exercised by the family in its selection of a place of worship. The pedestrian was loath to walk more than a mile to church. The horse and buggy was not good for more than three miles. Today, however, many people drive ten or more miles to the church of their choice. A Detroit church reports that only eighteen percent of its members live within five miles of the church building. In the past, many churches enjoyed what might be called "captive congregations" of people who could not conveniently go anywhere else. The present privilege of choice between many churches means that the only way to build up a constituency is to offer people something they distinctly want. One of the effects of this trend is that small churches tend to get smaller, and large ones larger.

Another effect is the fact that it is becoming increasingly hazardous to send small children to church school by themselves. Practically all children under ten are now brought to the church.

As families travel greater distances to the church of their choice, they are less likely to take the children to the church school, go back and get them, and return a third time to attend services. The trend is for all of the family to go together in one trip. In the South and in many parts of the West, the practice is for all ages to go to the church school—and then home. In the East and North, increasing numbers of churches schedule school classes for at least the younger children at the same hour as the church service. In either case this calls for more space. (Parallel sessions of the church school and of church worship, it must be pointed out, also require a degree of sound separation which in many old buildings can only be achieved with great difficulty.)

The most spectacular difference which the automobile has made in church life is the need for parking. As one minister puts it, "We must park the car before we can pew its passengers." Cars get bigger and more numerous all the time—and arrive at church with fewer persons in them. If a family has two cars, both are likely to turn up at church!

The safety factor is becoming increasingly important. The practice of the past was to locate churches on the most conspicuous corners—right where we have the most traffic today, as well as the greatest physical hazards! Particularly objectionable is the common practice of driving to the church, letting the children out for church school, and then returning ahead of time and parking double, often on the opposite side of the street, until the children emerge from the building and make their way through traffic to the waiting car. It is more likely good fortune, rather than proper precaution, which has held down the number of traffic accidents in front of churches. The only long-range answer to this problem is to provide for the arrival and departure of all car-driven churchgoers off the highway, in adequate church parking space.

Outside of the larger cities, most churches are confronted by three possibilities: they can acquire or arrange for parking at their present location; they can move to a new location where adequate off-street parking is available; they can ignore the parking problem and be slowly strangled by the increasing difficulty which new people will experience in coming to them. Lack of adequate parking is a minor deterrent to those whose relationship to a church is well established, but it is a major hindrance to the newcomer who has not committed himself and is therefore free to go somewhere else.

A fact which most church people are reluctant to face is that the majority of our existing buildings are more or less obsolete. An occasional old church has been so well planned that all it may now need is additional rooms; but this is the exception. Between 1931 and 1946, practically no churches were built. Most pre-World War II churches are from twenty-five to seventy-five years old—and were built when American architecture was at its lowest ebb. It is inevitable that most of them should be poorly suited to the needs of today.

Their deficiencies are evident in several ways. Structurally, they suffer from many flaws. At the worst they are unsafe; at the best, expensive to maintain. Our fathers were addicted to curiously complicated roofs which leak at every opportunity, and to the multiplication of steps; on the other hand, they were perversely economical when it came to the width of entrances.

Another difficulty is that since most of our churches were built, the functions which they serve have changed radically. This is seen most dramatically where churches have acquired parking lots at the side or rear of the church building; congregations now come and go through doors which were designed for the delivery of groceries into the kitchen. The facilities for the church school are limited; for church parlors and church offices, frequently non-existent.

Many churches are also theologically obsolete. Almost always the architecture of a building reflects the beliefs of the people who worship in it. The theological uncertainties, the growing pains of the past have bequeathed us many nondescript churches. Some are quaint, others are cozy, many are frankly out to impress the neighbors, but few offer any testimony to the faith of their builders. Today there is an insistent demand that a religious building have a religious message incarnated in its physical structure.

As a congregation faces the considerations we have outlined, it should reach a definite decision. The decision may be to move to a new location. It may be to expand and modernize existing facilities. Or the members may decide to keep their church where it is pretty much "as is." This may be a laudable decision, but it may merely be a lazy one. Too many churches remain where they are because members lack the mental and spiritual stamina to face the realities of their situation, or the energy to change them.

A word may be in order regarding the congregation which decides "to stay and serve the people of the neighborhood." If it is intelligently arrived at, this can be a noble decision. However, a number of prior questions must be asked: Are there needs which this church can meet? (If a neighborhood has gone Polish, there is little a Protestant church can realistically achieve in that neighborhood.) Is there any other church which meets or could meet these needs more effectively? Is the character of the congregation such that it will welcome and absorb people of a different background? Is there money available to support the work this church should do for the next ten years? Is the building suited to the activities that should be carried on? Has the leadership sufficient imagination to walk in new ways and seek new ends?

If a congregation can answer most of these questions affirmatively, it can serve the Kingdom of God where it is. However, even this decision may require at least the tidying up of the building; it may call for extensive alterations. It is hardly possible to serve a new constituency without making some visible adaptations. A striking example of this is the Horace Bushnell Church of Hartford, Connecticut. This congregation conceived of itself as the responsible stronghold of Protestantism serving the northern portion of the city. It took the proceeds brought by a merging congregation, and added to it a considerable sum of new money, to tear down the old mansion which had formerly housed the educational and social work of the church, and erected a modern structure in its stead. With ample parking, a friendly entrance, and adequate facilities, it can calmly face the changes the future may bring. More decisions like this one are needed. Blessed is the church that stays put, provided that it knows what it is doing and has counted the cost.

In any event, considerable caution should be exercised in the way in which a building proposal is presented to a congregation. At the center of every church is a group of individuals who are familiar with its activities and aware of the problems which confront it. In general they are the members of the governing boards and the more important committees. Convincing *them* that something should be done in order to face the future more effectively is a comparatively easy matter. They "know the score." They are committed to the work of their church. They are in a position to consider intelligently the improvement of the present property, the building of a new church, even moving to a new location.

What must be remembered, however, is that they

are a minority of the congregation. Every church also has a scattering of members whose interest may be described as peripheral. Their parents may have been stanch members of the church; they themselves grew up in it. Their children attended the church school and may have been married before its altar. Now they attend on Sunday morning, but know or care little about what goes on during the week. Numerically this fringe usually outnumbers the devoted souls at the center.

If a premature vote is taken on building or moving, the chances are that those with only a casual interest will defeat it on grounds of sentiment, nostalgia for the past, sheer inertia, or the fear that the proposal may cost too much. The wise strategy is to avoid any decisive votes until all the factors in the situation have been placed before as many of the congregation as is possible. We distrust the snap judgment of any group, but we have complete confidence in the democratic process when the people really know what they are doing. For this reason the preliminary votes should be to survey the situation, to explore possibilities—even to find out how much money can be raised—rather than to move or to build. Final action on the fundamental issues should be postponed as long as possible.

A "wait and see" approach will avoid much trouble. We once went to a church whose members were set on calling a business meeting to "decide" two critical matters: whether or not to have a basement, and what style of architecture should be followed—all this before the real problem of where to put the building had even been studied! The congregation was divided into pro-basement and anti-basement groups, and was now getting ready to take sides for and against a "colonial" church. We explained that these were not the first but the *last* questions, and that the placement of the building on the site would probably settle them. The meeting was deferred, and peace prevailed.

A congregation should not be asked to vote on any matter until it really knows what it is voting about. Many a worth-while building proposal has been killed because it was presented prematurely to an uninformed congregation. The purpose of this book is to show how a congregation can be led to an intelligent decision.

Chapter **2**

PROBLEMS AND POSSIBILITIES

THIS is a grand and awful time for churches to build.
Never before were more delightful results to be
achieved, nor more difficulties to be faced.

The obvious problems are financial. Costs have not
merely risen; they have multiplied. This has not been
a simple across-the-line boost. The prices of materials
have soared, and the cost of labor has zoomed. From
rural Missouri comes this observation: "These stone
buildings were erected by men who received $2.50 a
day; the last work we had done cost $3.50 an *hour*!"

The rising cost of labor has had two effects on church
building.

Changing old buildings or even adding to them has
become increasingly uneconomic. A carpenter put it
graphically: "In remodeling you pull out two nails to
drive in one, and it takes more time and effort to get
an old one out than to put a new one in!" Any addition
to an old building immediately takes on the age of the
original structure. A wing can rarely be salvaged when

a main structure is razed. Our fathers were accustomed to cheap labor, and consequently remodeled both their houses and their churches from time to time with what we could call reckless abandon. Such practices do not make sense today. Altering, adding, rebuilding in the old way are no longer economically feasible.

The current hourly wage rates also discourage both the elaborate decorations and the adherence to traditional architectural styles which characterize most old churches. The patches of "gingerbread," the turrets and towers, the windows with round and pointed tops, the Gothic buttresses and the Georgian columns have all become impossibly expensive. The essential framework of a church has become so costly that there is little money left over for frills of any sort.

Those who desire to follow the patterns of the past will find that this is indeed a terrible time to build a church. Even were we anxious to reproduce what our fathers did, we lack the means to do so. Economic necessity compels us to walk in new paths. The first step toward a new church is for the congregation to be prepared to relinquish old ideas. It cannot cling too fondly to the Christmas-card image of a stately stone edifice with light shining through stained glass windows upon the snow.

Only the congregation willing to face the new can discover the multiple and alluring building possibilities brought to us by modern construction techniques. The present way of handling steeples illustrates what is happening in building generally. The heavenward-pointing fingers which are the glory of New England were put together piece by piece by steeplejacks working on lofty scaffolds—a costly process. Their current counter-parts are made of aluminum or steel cast at the mill, easily assembled on the ground, and then elevated to their perch by a gigantic hoist. In rural North Carolina it took a crew just one hour to put a steeple in place. For this the charge was $250, a bargain in view of the methods of the past.

The men who built the world's great cathedrals would be overjoyed at the prospect of using methods now available to us. Consider the problem of roof sup-ports, as one example. Medieval builders had to pile stone on stone to get a wall that could carry the weight; then they added buttresses to take care of the outward thrust produced by the weight of the roof. Today we have materials—both metal and wood—which, weigh-ing little themselves, nevertheless carry surprising loads. The result is a considerably lighter structure re-quiring much less in the way of a foundation.

Exterior walls which once had the thickness of a for-tress are now little more than a lightweight skin. Where our fathers laid stone, we pour concrete. Old churches commonly have dungeon-like cavities beneath them, with a forest of posts or pillars supporting the floor of the church. Today we lay our cement floors right on the ground—and let the good earth hold them up.

With new ways of building have come startling new materials. Of these the most dramatic are the laminated wood arches used for roof supports. They are composed of layers of plywood glued together and bent to the proper curve before the glue (which is even stronger than the wood!) has set. These arches have several ad-vantages. Although relatively light, they can take a heavy load. All that is needed by way of foundation is a good footing for each arch. Their delivery time is usually less than that for steel. Their insurance rate is lower. When steel gets hot it crumples, but laminated wood arches merely char.

Although the arches represent a real financial investment, they are actually economical because, as the sole support of the roof, they eliminate the need for other construction. They can be curved, as in Quonset hut construction, or brought to a point. Whether pointed or round, they are always gracefully symmetrical. The laminated wood arch is giving churches the upthrust which was the inspiring feature of Gothic architecture, but now the arch is purely and completely functional.

Many new churches, wisely enough, have few if any plastered surfaces. Expensive both to build and to maintain, plastered walls require frequent attention. Instead, churches are now using brick or block. Brick has a ruddy color suggesting rugged strength. Block walls are commonly a light gray, but can be painted any color desired. The block is frequently left in its natural state in the place of worship, while corridors and educational areas are often attractively colored. Some people may feel that brick and block are cold and unduly austere, but the fact is that both can serve as excellent backgrounds for warm, rich colors in hangings or window drapes. In the Church of the Good Shepherd in Minneapolis, a brick wall affords a perfect setting for the silhouette of the Good Shepherd which dominates the room.

Glass is an old material which is finding increasing uses in new churches. When used in large sheets, it is less costly than a solid wall. Glass may be more expensive than brick or block for the same area, but its ease of installation permits certain savings. The greatest use of glass is in educational and social rooms, and at the entrances to churches, where many gracious effects are produced. Plate glass rather than thermopane is used widely in churches and schools, since there is little moisture to produce condensation. In theory, considerable heat is lost through glass; we have found, however, that in both schools and churches, the complaint is not about cold coming in, but about the discomfort which develops when the sun shines directly on the glass. In old churches the drafts around windows are caused far more by cracks around the frame and in the leading than by any fault of the glass. Glass bricks are also beginning to appear in churches, with interesting results. The churches of the future will surely have in them far more glass, and also far more light, than did those of the past.

Today's trend in church building reveals a shift from vertical to horizontal lines—a change wrought by the need for larger sites with more parking space, by concern for the safety of small children, and by awareness of the difficulty older people have in climbing. The one-story church, with the floor right on the ground, is the most functional and economical way to build. Moreover, the spread-out church permits vistas which were impossible with the piled-up structures of the past. There can be gardens and patios; the outdoors and the indoors can blend. Church garden clubs, a novelty now, may well be commonplace in the future.

The adaptation of a church to its physical environment calls for more thought than has been customary in our past. The frame churches of New England have withstood winter's blast and summer's sun for two centuries or even more; but the same structures crack up under the California sun in a few years—explaining the dearth of "colonial" churches in our fastest-growing state. In the Pacific Northwest it rains much of the time; and church members seek to catch what sunbeams they can by using much glass in their places of worship. In the Southwest, the sun is more of an enemy than a friend, and we find the Spanish style of building ingeniously designed to hold interior sunlight to a minimum. In the South, however, the adaptation of church architecture to climatic conditions has made little headway. Most of the churches in Florida would be equally appropriate in Kalamazoo; the South needs churches which will reflect its way of life.

The same may be said for other sections of the country. On the flat plains do steeples belong? In hilly country how effective are spread-out churches? Actually there are no generally accepted patterns for churches, and this is particularly true of educational and parish buildings. There is surprisingly little that anyone would care to copy. For the timid this may be a problem; for the venturesome it is an invitation. Never before has there been so much need for congregations to dedicate their thinking and especially their imagination to planning places of worship. Never before has there been so much interest in the church as an *institution*. Never before has there been so much intelligence enlisted in its service, on the part of lay people as well as architects. Out of the impossibility of copying the past and the challenge of meeting different needs, a new utility and a new beauty, we believe, will emerge.

The following chapters will deal in more detail with the multitudinous problems involved in building churches today. Purposely we will refrain from offering specific plans; instead we will present problems and suggest ways in which they may be attacked. Our hope is that this approach will stimulate congregations to do their own creative thinking.

Chapter **3**

IF WE MOVE

Most of the new churches which will be built in this country during the next few years will be on new locations. A few fortunate congregations occupy prominent landmarks from which they should never move. These are largely in New England, where the first churches were established at the center of the community; that was and is logical. But throughout most of the country the majority of churches would welcome any excuse to move somewhere else.

Three practical considerations lead a congregation to look for a new site. In the long view the most compelling of these is the lack of adequate off-street parking, although the full import of this is as yet rarely recognized. A second effective reason is the dilapidation of the old building. Repairs and alterations are increasingly expensve. People are loath to sink their money in an old building in the wrong location. But the consideration which is most likely to lead to action is a good offer for the property. Congregations enjoy real estate deals, especially when they appear to be advantageous financially.

In attempting a relocation, one of the first questions to be raised will be: to whom can we sell our present holdings?

If your church is on a main thoroughfare near the heart of the community, this will be no problem, although congregations so located often cling to their sites for sentimental reasons. If you are within a block of the shopping district and you occupy a sizable area, conceivably you could sell it to the city for a parking lot. The survival of much centrally located business depends upon parking, and in many communities the merchants are putting the heat on the city fathers to provide it for them. To sell under such circumstances is to perform an appreciated civic service. From such a deal the Congregational Church in Austin, Minnesota, realized $100,000.

If your church is between the business center and a residential area, it will not be so readily salable. Undertakers are sometimes interested in such locations, but the likeliest prospects are other churches. These fall into two groups, racial and evangelistic.

The Negroes are the best customers for broken-down churches, which is unfortunate, as they often get little but trouble for their money. Much shrewder buyers are the Greeks, who do an astonishing job when they fix up an old church. Other language groups offer some possibilities.

The more zealously evangelistic groups, such as the Church of the Nazarene, the Christian and Missionary Alliance, the various branches of the Church of God, and the Pentecostal groups are looking for old churches. One congregation helped out its six neighboring churches so far as parking is concerned by selling to the Seventh-day Adventists.

Fortunately the people who attend these churches are apparently not as wedded to their cars as are the older generations of Americans—at least they will walk further from a parking place to the church door, and they are not averse to climbing when they get there. They like the auditorium-type church, and are not troubled by the lack of facilities for small children and for social activities.

Getting from the old site to a new location is a far more complicated process than most people realize. You can't just go out and buy a lot.

The rights and wishes of other churches must be respected. It is no longer proper for a congregation to move where it pleases without taking thought for its sister churches. The familiar sight of churches on opposite corners or crowded into the same block together must not be repeated. Churches gain immensely as they succeed in keeping out of each other's way.

In most metropolitan areas the council of churches undertakes to guide the placing of churches through its comity committee. If a congregation desires to move into a new section, a hearing is held at which existing churches can state their objections, if any, to the new location. Some ministers have rather fanciful ideas as to the geographical extent of their sphere of influence, but the genuine interests of the other churches should be respected. This takes time and may be exasperating, but the result is to give a congregation a clear field on which the other cooperating denominations represented in the council of churches will not trespass. Unfortunately the churches on the extremes, both theologically and liturgically, do not usually have any dealings with councils of churches, and reserve the right to do as they please even when it involves moving into an area which has already been assigned to some other church. However, their appeal is to limited groups rather than to the community as a whole, and their competition is rarely serious.

We suspect that most of the re-locations of the immediate future will be in communities too small to support an active council of churches. We foresee in cities from 5,000 to 50,000 in population a general exodus of churches from the center toward the periphery because of parking difficulties and the general obsolescence of existing structures. In such situations every congregation which moves out makes matters that much easier for those remaining, particularly with parking, so their departure will be generally welcome. In this process there should be some friendly counseling among churches to make certain that they do not all move in the same direction.

Comity is only one of the hurdles which must be negotiated in moving toward a new site. The better a residential area, the more severe the restrictions under which land is usually sold; and churches are commonly rated as undesirable neighbors, at least by the real estate people. In an old community a strong church helps to stabilize values, but promoters and salespeople do not see that far ahead. There have been court decisions discouraging the specific restriction against churches, but that does not free them from the general considerations under which land is sold. In most cities there are zoning ordinances which must be taken into account. We know of several places where it has been necessary to get a release from the neighbors before a church could be built.

We have some suggestions at this point. If there is a city planner or a local planning commission, they should be consulted in the beginning. It is their business to know what the population trends are and what new developments may be expected, all of which a church needs to take into account. If he had his way, the average city planner would like to use churches as buffers between business areas and residential sections, which is not a bad idea. The cooperation of the planning authorities can be most helpful. In any case a direct collision should be avoided. We have been told by city planners that many of the difficulties which churches encounter in re-locating are due to poor public relations. In some cities it is necessary to hold a public hearing if anybody objects to the granting of a building permit for a church, and this is an invitation for trouble-makers. A church coming into a new community needs to cultivate good will. It should make clear what its resources are and that what it builds will be an asset rather than a liability to the neighborhood. The greatest objection people have to living next to churches is the matter of parking. They fear that their driveway may be blocked by cars, and they know that the ordinary policeman is slow to enforce the law on anyone who seems to be bound for church. A rather curious secondary objection is that some people think all churches are noisy. The best answer to neighborhood objections is to assure everyone that the site is large enough so that there will be plenty of offstreet parking, and the building will be back far enough so that choir practice will not disturb the neighbors.

On top of these considerations, the congregation itself may have some ideas on where it would like to go and what it would choose to be near! The principles for locating churches in large metropolitan areas have been rather carefully worked out, but primarily on a pedestrian rather than a motor-car basis. Although people move out from the city, it is easier to draw them back toward the city rather than out, for church. For this reason a church should be on the inner side of the area which it seeks to serve. It should be on or near a main thoroughfare which really leads somewhere. It should keep away from population barriers such as railroad tracks, rivers, parks, cemeteries, and large industrial plants, and should seek instead a location where it can draw from all directions. Nearness to a grade school is helpful, but junior and senior high schools are no asset, probably because the young people who attend them come from a large area and likely already have their church affiliations.

Frequently, congregations have selected sites which, they said in delight, were "just what we wanted"— only to find that the land could not be bought; others, still more unfortunate, have secured the land but were then denied the right to build on it. While either situation produces dismay, the end result has often been that the members looked further and found something really better suited to their needs. Incidentally, this is one way in which a group can be led to move a greater distance than it was originally willing to consider; and the future, we find, is usually better served by the long jump. Locations which are at first passed by rather casually may in the end prove to be the best choice. The search for a new site should be far-ranging and thorough: no possibility should be overlooked.

To live and grow, a church must be related to a group of people. It must have either a present or a prospective constituency. This may be based either on geographical propinquity or social congeniality or, more often than not, a combination of the two.

When the country was first settled, parishes had to be geographical simply because people had no good way of getting about. You had to go to the church you could get to. Unfortunately, people who live close together do not always agree or even like each other. The inability of one church to suit everybody, combined with the limited area which it could serve, helped give birth to the multitude of small, competing, sectarian churches which is the curse of Protestantism in many communities today.

The rise of the automobile, however, has greatly helped this situation. The people who do not like the church next door no longer have to start another one; they can drive on down the road to one of which they approve. Because of the mobility of the American people, church attendance is becoming increasingly selective. Most congregations are no longer composed of neighbors but of like-minded people drawn from many miles around.

Into this picture the real estate developers have introduced another element. The way lots are now sold, the people who live in a particular block are likely to have approximately the same income. The American people are being sorted out by economic levels. In a general way people who have the same size pocketbooks tend to think in similar ways. The community life which the automobile shattered is being somewhat restored by our realtors.

These considerations have a bearing on the selection of a site for a church.

A new congregation of an inclusive denomination (Methodist, Presbyterian, Congregational, etc.) will usually expect to recruit its constituency on a geographical basis. It will make a community appeal. For that reason a prime consideration is to locate where there will be a group of people susceptible to the appeal of a "standard brand" Protestant church within a convenient distance.

All old congregations, and even new ones of denominations with a less inclusive appeal (Lutheran, Episcopal, and some Fundamentalist groups) gather their people on a selective basis. They can assume that a certain number of people, either because of old ties or theological convictions, will seek them out, even though it involves traveling quite a distance. Of course many of these congregations will hope to pick up some local adherents on the basis of proximity, but they are not dependent upon them for success. Whether we like it or not, our Protestant churches are becoming increasingly selective in their followings. General accessibility is more important to most churches than the community immediately about them.

While all of these considerations should be borne in mind, the paramount question, at least for an old congregation seeking a new location, is, "Will the proposed site permit us to do the things we will need to do?" Forced to choose between an acre-and-a-half site and one twice that size a mile further from the center of town, we would prefer the latter. Most people now drive to church and are not likely to change their habits. Once the car is started, a mile or two more or less does not make much difference. With the abundance of cars now available, transportation can be arranged for those who still travel on foot. Except in the largest cities, dependence upon public transportation is a delusion. Buses are ceasing to run on Sunday in community after community simply because nobody cares to ride on them. The more thoroughly a congregation accepts the automobile, the better off it will be in the long run.

In an increasing number of cities and even states, off-street parking is becoming a legal requirement as well as a practical necessity for churches. The law on such matters is bound to become more stringent. A church in Toledo, Ohio, which had lost its building by fire, was refused a permit for a new structure because of the lack of parking space. When a church on Long Island with parking for 225 cars proposed to enlarge its educational facilities, it was told that no permit would be forthcoming unless more parking was provided.

The ratio of seats in a church to parking places outside is declining. The first laws were lenient, requiring one car space for ten seats on the inside, but this has gotten down to a proportion of four to one for at least one city in Southern California. This is as it should be.

Church attendance is increasing, but most cars come to church lightly loaded. When the church school is at a separate hour, the average may be as low as one and a half persons per car; with church school at the same hour as church, this may double.

Lack of parking space may ultimately be suicidal. The city planner of Los Angeles has declared that one of his worst problems is the small church with a small parking lot which prospers and wants to expand on to the parking area for church school rooms. Some congregations have paid fancy prices for parking lots. We know of large churches in Minneapolis and Los Angeles which are buying up adjacent property in self-protection. What good is a million-dollar edifice if there is no place for prospective worshipers to leave their cars?

Wherever possible, the church of the future will be all on one floor. As later pages will point out, both the number and variety of rooms needed by a congregation are increasing. The best legacy we can leave the future is room in which to expand.

To do these things adequately will take a lot of land. We were present when a small church on the coast of Maine bought a ten-acre site. We know of several old congregations which have secured five or six acres. Once we met for a couple of hours with a new congregation in North Carolina which had been given two acres. The group tried to work out the location for a parking lot, an educational building and a future place of worship in this area, and ended by asking for another acre. Two acres is about the minimum for a church and parking lot, with more much to be preferred.

Where can such tracts be secured?

In our larger cities they can rarely be had. Here the best strategy for the churches is to throw in their lot with the local merchants, who face the same problem. One solution is to persuade the city to establish public parking lots. Another is to secure the use of supermarket lots for evenings and Sundays. Here the difficulty is that no assurance of permanent tenure can be obtained.

For cities of 100,000 or under there are two possibilities.

Old mansions surrounded by considerable land can sometimes be had. These properties are often a burden to their present owners and a threat to their heirs, who may be confronted with an inheritance tax out of proportion to the utility or salability of the property. Such bequests to one's children are a doubtful blessing. The Roman Catholic Church has capitalized on many situations of this sort. In Salamanca, New York, the Congregational church purchased the town showplace, including a small park, for $20,000. Unfortunately, such opportunities are disappearing.

The other alternative has already been suggested—move to the edge of town, or even beyond.

Will the people follow? In a few years we will have much evidence on this point. What is now available suggests an emphatic Yes! Way back in 1930 the First Baptist Church of Cleveland moved out beyond the end of the car line and has prospered immensely. In 1952 the First Congregational Church of Clinton, Iowa, migrated from a century-old site on Main Street to an 18-acre tract on a hill overlooking the city. Although it was necessary to put in a rather steep road, and the congregation was able to erect only an educational building, the attendance and financial support increased greatly.

Moving out practically always enhances the visibility of a church. In the center of town it is usually overshadowed by other buildings, and may have to compete with show windows for attention. Whether on foot or in cars most people hurry past, and consequently have hazy notions as to which is which. But put a church out on the highway where it is free from competition, and give it any distinction whatever, and the public will soon know where it is.

Once a site is secured, it should be studied carefully.

A church is a public building seeking public attention. Every site has what might be called its psychological center, which a church should capitalize to the utmost. If the land slopes, this may be its highest point. If there are any curves in the approaching highways there may be a spot which is emphatically at the head of the street. Or possibly if the roads were continued there is a place where they would meet or cross. At this strategic point the church should ultimately erect a commanding symbol—steeple, tower, belfry. Where this belongs should be the first decision concerning the use of the land.

The placing of the other buildings should be worked out in relation to two foci—the dominant symbol and the parking area. The buildings should be related to the parking lot rather than to the street. It should be assumed that most people will drive to church, and that they will park their car and then take the shortest route possible to the place of worship or to the church school or social rooms, as the case may be.

Before any plans are prepared, a general scheme of land use should be worked out. This should not be too detailed. There is no likelihood of any master plan's proving completely satisfactory to those who are directing the church ten years from now. We cannot foresee the details of future needs. The best that we can do is to keep out of the way of further developments. This means allotting areas so that there will be plenty of room for whatever our successors may want to do. The first units should not sprawl all over the place.

Yet the emphasis should be on separateness rather than togetherness. In the past the conventional plan for a church has been an L or a T with the educational and social rooms opening off the pulpit end of the church. This has promoted confusion where quiet was most desired and has made for awkwardness in other ways. A better arrangement is to have the rooms for worship, education, and social life fan out from a common entrance, as has been done in striking fashion in the Church of St. Peter and St. Paul in Cincinnati.

A further step is to think of a church as a group of buildings rather than as one great structure. This is known as the campus-style church. A good example is the Oneonta Congregational Church of South Pasadena, California. The advantages are complete sound separation, the elimination of traffic jams, the ease with which additional units can be built as they are needed. The argument against this arrangement is that people must go outside to get from one place to another, and that this is undesirable in cold climates. By way of rebuttal it can be said that the amount of passing to and fro in the modern church is much less than is commonly assumed. Children are taken to their quarters and then met there after the church school is over. Women who come for a tea have nothing to do with the place of worship. Colonnades to keep off the rain, or even covered passageways, may be desirable where the climate is rugged. We believe that the future will see more churches of this type.

Chapter **4**

FIRST COMES PARKING

MANY church boards fear the subject of parking—and, fearing it, develop an ostrich-like attitude. "We have no problem," is frequently their response. Or, "It isn't really serious." Or, "We're no worse off than everybody else around here."

These answers all dodge the question. Church boards may not even know there *is* a question. Officers arrive at the building early; they know where good spots for parking are to be found; indeed, they may not be averse to walking a short distance. For them parking is merely an incidental irritation. But the newcomer or the less deliberate church member arrives late, drives around a couple of blocks looking for a space, and comes in exasperated during the middle of the service. Unless the minister can pass a miracle, that newcomer will not hurry back the following Sunday!

Here are two fundamental facts about church parking.

First, our streets are being increasingly restricted to

vehicles which are in motion. In front of our older churches, therefore, the progression is from parking on one side only (usually the wrong side), to metered parking, to no parking whatever. These regulations create more difficulties for weekday meetings than for Sunday worship.

Second, the church which has an abundance of off-street parking will automatically enjoy a great advantage over the church which does not. Just as with business establishments, any institutions seeking to attract people today must provide a place for their cars.

We will assume that all newly located churches will have parking facilities and that many churches which remain where they are will provide them. The principles which follow will apply fully to the new church, and in varying degrees to old ones.

The first problem is to get the cars of prospective churchgoers out of traffic. This writer, a fairly cautious driver, has nevertheless repeatedly overshot churches he was trying to reach, and also remembers having made some mighty quick turns which could have been hazardous. The approach to a church should be well marked, and far enough in advance so that a driver can get into the proper lane and slow down before he reaches the turn. To alert him, signs which can be seen and read at a speed of 50 miles an hour—*not* the timid sort of sign to which many congregations seem addicted —should be posted.

If possible, the entrance to a church parking area should be accessible from side streets, rather than from main highways, with the turns in and out of traffic at an established, regulated intersection. This means that the turns must be well marked on both the main route and the side road.

If church parking facilities are to be effective, they must be clearly visible. Assurance that one's car will have a parking space can be potent encouragement to church attendance, but newcomers will respond to this strong inducement only if they can see it. The sight of churches surrounded by lanes of gleaming cars is disturbing to the consciences of the Sunday golfers and fishermen who may go whizzing by. A large part of the population needs to be impressed by the example of those who are going to church. Some architects feel that parking lots are by nature ugly, and should be concealed behind the church. With this we disagree emphatically. Parking areas need not be eyesores; when they are filled with modern cars in a rainbow of colors they present an impressive sight.

Driveways leading in and out of church parking areas should be one-way. While this is only mildly important during the week, on Sunday morning it is essential. Otherwise, those who are going home from one service will tangle with those who are arriving for another—whether it be church school and church, or two church services paralleled by church-school sessions.

Whenever possible these drives should be so laid out that unloading and loading is from the right side of the car into the church entrances. This convenience will be of primary importance to children and older people, since they most of all must be able to get out of the car without next facing the hazard of crossing into traffic.

A church-bound car can either unload and then park, or park before unloading. We know of a Roman Catholic church which has established separate lanes for these two types of traffic. We also know of Protestant churches which have provided elaborate porte-cocheres and loading platforms, only to have them seldom used. What apparently happens is that the boys and girls and the older folk are left at the appropriate door all right, but then a man and wife or an older person with a small child will park the car and walk back. (We have seen churches where this was a highly social process.) For this reason the parking should be as convenient as possible to the ultimate destination of those who come. Thought should also be given to providing ample entrances from the parking lot. Often elaborate entrances from the street are little used, while the small doors provided for car drivers are overcrowded. Parking should also be decentralized. Instead of one big parking field, smaller areas convenient to various entrances are preferable. This is particularly helpful during the week.

The most efficient use of parking can be made only when the area is hard-surfaced and properly marked. For the new church just getting on its feet, this may be a financial burden. One of the advantages of building a relatively small place of worship and offering the congregation the choice of two worship services is that this also reduces the parking space which the local authorities may require. Money can be saved, too, by physically treating different parts of the lot in different ways. Where cars are parked regularly on weekdays, there should be a pavement. Areas which are used chiefly on Sunday can be inexpensively blacktopped. A portion of the plot could be left as field for very occasional use, such as Easter, when parking lots reflect the overflow crowds. Or, since the ground may be wet and soggy at that time of year, a gravel top might better be used.

Much thought should be given to the parking lot arrangement. Church lots differ from those of shopping centers, in that a congregation comes and goes over a limited period of time. For this reason field parking, which serves well for stores, would produce troublesome bottlenecks for churches. The best layout is probably a one-way shoestring with angle parking. This should make any prolonged delays impossible.

The angle at which cars should be parked will depend fundamentally upon the width of the available area and how it can best be divided. It is commonly assumed that right-angle parking will accommodate the most cars; but it must be pointed out that this is not necessarily a clear-cut advantage. Ninety-degree parking on both sides of the roadway requires an aisle of twenty-two feet on either side, or a total width of sixty-two feet. On the other hand, thirty-degree parking calls for only a ten-foot aisle, and seventeen feet on either side, or a total width of forty-four feet. This will not take as many cars per acre as right-angle parking, but it is easier to get in and out of, and may be better suited to the size of the parking area. The best arrangement should be worked out for a given situation—and the stalls clearly marked. See the illustration on the next page for the effect of parking angles.

A parking lot will not run itself. Lot attendants are even more important than ushers within the church. Supervision will keep down confusion and possible ac-

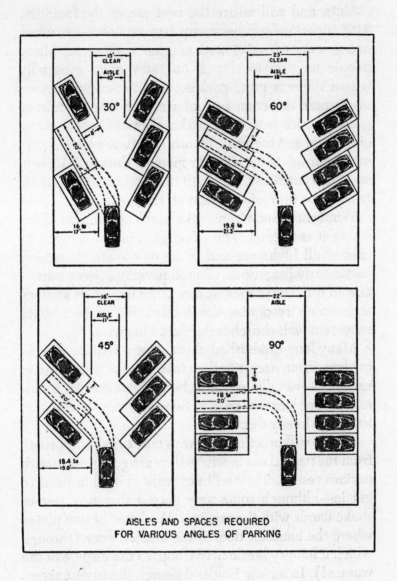

AISLES AND SPACES REQUIRED
FOR VARIOUS ANGLES OF PARKING

cidents, and will assure the best use of the facilities. This is particularly necessary between services, when one group is leaving and another coming in. Many people now go to church on rainy days, especially where there is good parking, but these churchgoers need more direction in foul weather than in fair. A good practice is to have parking committees of six or eight men serving for a month at a time under a permanent head. Some should report for duty at 9:15, say, and others at 10:30. By 11:10 they can stow away their equipment to rejoin the church service.

Wintertime snow removal should be contracted for where it is needed. The effect of a fall of snow is to narrow all highways and make on-the-street parking particularly hazardous. Church parking is more important in the winter than at any other time. Gas stations and motels recognize the importance of immediate snow removal; churches should do likewise.

Many long-established churches are acquiring parking lots. From necessity they take them where they can get them—usually beside or behind the existing building. Either location creates two problems, in addition to those already discussed.

People will practically always take the shortest route from the parked car to where they are going, often with curious results. They will not walk around in front to get in—although some may go out that way just to shake hands with the minister. We know of two places where the handiest door is the kitchen door (through which a hungry horde may troop, to the disgust of the women!). In a New England church the easiest access is through the old woodshed, past a primitive men's toilet, through the Sunday school room, and upstairs into church. Often the backdoor thus becomes the main entrance. The virtue in this development is that instead of being pushed out the front door of the church like toothpaste out of a tube, the congregation filters back through several rooms on their way to their cars, with considerable social intercourse as they move along. Nevertheless, old churches with new parking areas can profitably give thought to the improvement of their parking lot entrances and the route from the lot into the church.

When a church opens a parking lot in a built-up area it faces the problem of illicit squatters on its property. Charging fees would not produce enough income to pay an attendant, while it might get the land on the tax roll. Some churches supply their members with windshield stickers designed to sort out the saints from the sinners. In a certain New England city, the First Parish church enjoys what other congregations regard as an unfair advantage, in that its members have the privilege of weekday parking right in the heart of the city as a rather valuable dividend on their church relationship. A common practice is to wink at weekday interlopers but to put up chains across the entrances on Saturday and at other times when the space is needed for church people.

Chapter 5

WOOING THE MULTITUDE IN

A CHURCH can do little for people until they have first passed through its doors. It should therefore be easy to enter. It should catch the eye, stir the imagination, and woo the feet of all who pass by. It should, in a word, be winsome.

This may well begin with the name. Few people will tempt fate in an anonymous place of worship. At the least they want to make sure that they are not going astray and joining the followers of some strange cult. They will usually ascertain the designation of a church before pushing open its doors. Yet most church names are utterly unexciting. We have an astronomical number of "First" churches, and too many "Second's." Real estate subdivisions, streets, and points of the compass figure prominently in our ecclesiastical nomenclature.

If you are starting a new church, or moving an old one to a new location, why not give it a name with some distinctiveness? Good names are scarce, but they are also priceless. Why accept the commonplace just because it is convenient? Why not tax somebody's brain with the task of finding a good name?

Once a unique designation is discovered, it should be blazoned to the world. Most conventional signs are worthless. One of my jobs is to find churches. Trying to read their names while driving is to invite traffic jams, if not accidents. Our fathers associated Gothic lettering with God and assumed that there was something holy about illegibility. Most of the time I let myself be guided by the architecture rather than try to decipher the label.

Today the most effective kind of church sign is a frank imitation of those displayed by the gas stations. It should be at right angles to traffic, lettered on both sides, elevated above the highway, as close to the curb as the authorities will permit, and illuminated at night. It should be designed primarily for ease of reading. The name of the church and the hour of worship are all that a motorist will notice, and they are quite sufficient. A Protestant church in Lowell, Massachusetts, has protected its sign from desecration by placing on it two little crosses. This might be described as protective coloration for some localities.

How an entrance should be handled depends upon where it is.

If a church faces a busy city street, the doorway is the one symbol that the public will see as they pass by. In crowded quarters it can do far more than a steeple to attract the eye, as people do not star-gaze from busy sidewalks.

A church door should be inviting. It should say "Come in!" emphatically. The best way to achieve this is by a liberal use of glass. Our storekeepers have found that a clear view of an attractive interior will get them more customers than the fanciest of show windows. We believe that one of the greatest hindrances to getting people through the doors of a church is their inability to see what they are getting into. In Madison, Wisconsin, an Episcopal church has been built after the manner of a Quonset hut, with the entire front of glass. The passer-by can actually pause on the sidewalk and see the entire service, which we hold is good for his soul. Glass doors also have utility. We were once leaving a church in New London, Connecticut, in the company of a captain in the United States Navy, at the same time that a woman was coming in laden with spaghetti. If there had not been glass in the door we would have knocked her and the spaghetti off the doorstep. A New Hampshire church is troubled by the town bums sitting on its steps. We contend that if the congregation painted the door frames white and installed glass, these gentlemen of leisure would take themselves elsewhere. If a church is unwilling to risk a door wholly of glass, we suggest as much glass as possible in a conventional door.

The door is to a church what a bull's eye is to a target. It is the spot where we want people to come. To this end it should be made distinctive. At night it should be bathed in light. The color of whatever wood there is in the door should be in striking contrast to its surroundings. Church doors should not be varnished, which soon discolors, but painted in bright hues. If the church is of gray stone, the door could be red; if of red brick, green; if white, blue. The eye should be caught by contrast. The paint should be frequently renewed. We know of a church which places in its budget every year an item for painting the doors. This is excellent public relations.

In the future we expect that an increasing number of churches will be entered from the parking lot rather than from the street. This poses an entirely different set of problems.

Church parking lots should be advertised in the public press, in the printed matter of the church, and by giving them maximum visibility.

How the entrance to church property should be dignified is a matter to which, as yet, little thought has been given. At night an abundance of light is desirable. Pillars, an arch, shrubbery may be in order. At the very least the matter should be given careful study.

The effect of a parking lot is to disperse rather than concentrate the traffic into a church. This is due in part to the area in which the cars are parked, and in part to the fact that church and church school are likely to meet at the same time, which means that the children must be taken to where their classes meet. This diffusion of movement, in turn, means that there should be several pathways, and that all of them should be marked showing how to get where, much as is sometimes done on a college campus. There are likely to be several ways into a newer type church.

In any case the approaches to the church should not be stiff and institutional but informal and human. In the past there has been too much emphasis on the big and imposing, especially on the outside. Within, the stairs and corridors have suggested a school house or some public institution. Today we desire the opposite impression. In many of its aspects a church should cultivate the atmosphere of a home.

On the outside this means the avoidance of wide stretches of walk and flights of steps such as are found on most state capitols. Instead there should be informal walks, not too wide (and on angles or curves rather than straight), and an abundance of shrubbery and flowers when possible.

The first impression on opening the door of a church should be one of happy surprise. I once went to preach in an old church which I had assumed was about to go out of business. On pulling open the door I was confronted with a table on which were some flowers and a lighted lamp, while beside it was an easy chair. Evidently someone loved the old church. I took courage.

The narthex to a church should be psychologically warm. The room should not appear stand-offish but should embrace those who enter. An old New England church was persuaded to paint its rather monumental entryway a Chinese red, "so that it would at least look warm." The result was unusual, but effective. The color scheme for this area may well be the reverse of the church proper. If the church is dark and mysterious, the entrance should be light and gay; if the church is white or near white, the narthex should be a rich, intimate color. In any case, it should say, "We're glad to see you. Relax and feel at home."

In a home, the hostess takes the wraps of her guests, and we suggest the same procedure for churches. In the Mother Church of Christian Science in Boston an attractive young woman takes your hat and coat and gives you a metal disc. When you come out, you put your check in a slot, and your things come bouncing up on a dumb waiter! Few churches can manage that, but a convenient coat room on the way into a church is something that most men will appreciate.

Before a church can do much for people, they must be persuaded to pass through its doors. Too much thought cannot be given to making this an easy and happy experience for them.

Chapter 6

SEEKING THE DIVINE PRESENCE

To BUILD all that is needed at once is impossible for new congregations, and difficult for old ones moving to new locations. Something must be postponed. Inevitably the question arises, Which shall we put up first, the church or the parish house?

At the outset the strongest pressures will favor the facilities which promise to be the most useful. To the ordinary layman, eating appears to be a more utilitarian activity than praying. Where to put the children who come to the church school seems more important than where to place the choir at church time. Most new church buildings are in new communities. Social facilities of all sorts are usually lacking. The new people who are flocking in want to get acquainted. The church is looked upon as a community convenience to be used by all and sundry. Some will rationalize the situation, arguing that by offering room for everybody to do most everything, the church will win the community and therefore become strong.

Unfortunately it does not work out in this way. For a few years the community-centered church which puts more emphasis on the community than on the church will be a busy place. It will be accepted as a neighborhood convenience. It will look successful because much will be happening. As time passes other institutions will appear, offering better facilities, and the weekday traffic through the doors of the church will decline. Community activities will not of themselves build a church, as has been often demonstrated. To shift the emphasis from social times to the worship of God is a most difficult operation.

Religious commitments are what build a church. Some support can be had for a community program, but the real money comes in on the offering plate on Sunday morning. The only other activities that pay their way are the church school and the women's society. Financially worship is the most profitable item on the program of a church. Often it must pay the bills for other seemingly more practical activities.

Congregations which have built the church first have made a stronger and more lasting impact upon their communities than those which have put their first investment in a parish house. To build a utilitarian basement in the hope of some day putting an ornamental church on top of it, has been a fatal mistake for many congregations. It has usually been a mistake to build something useful on the back of the lot. What people really want is a church that looks like a church and that behaves like a church. Neither the Lutherans nor the Episcopalians have bothered much with either Sunday schools or social doings, and yet they have prospered greatly in recent years. The voice of experience would seem to say, "Build the church first."

Yet these other needs are very real. A church must train its children. People need to meet for other than immediately religious purposes. A church cannot shut its doors in the face of its neighbors. Nor is this necessary.

The first concern should be to make the religious approach primary. After that is done, a number of accommodations can be worked out. In a new church the purchase of pews should be postponed. As long as the floor space can be used with some degree of flexibility, many things are possible. We once preached in an Episcopal church where the committee in charge later pulled the curtain in front of the altar, opened some windows in the rear, and proceeded to serve refreshments. We know of a congregation which for 25 years worshiped, ate, and even danced all in the same room, doing a remarkable job of scene-shifting for each occasion. The religious influence of pews has been greatly exaggerated. It is not what we sit on but what we see and hear which creates a religious mood.

Sometimes the opposite adaptation is made. We know of parish halls which are more worship-inspiring than many churches. Here the objection may be external. They do not look like a church to the passer-by. Sometimes the suggestion is that the religious emphasis is incidental to their appeal. A church should say "Church" emphatically and to all comers.

A dangerous procedure is to build a modest chapel against the day when an imposing church can be erected. This may block growth. The smaller the place of worship, the more courage it takes for the newcomer to venture in. He fears that he may be too conspicuous. Speaking of a room seating 90, which is large for a chapel, a friend testifies, "I was always afraid that the minister would reach out from the pulpit and put his hand on my head." A minister whose church seats about 150 rather smugly states, "The gospel operates at close quarters in our church. You either accept it and go along, or you stay away. The indifferent, the lukewarm just can't take it." A further difficulty with the chapel is that the congregation may become too content. Those who like it get attached to it, and there may be little disposition to make room for more.

The wise congregation will build first for worship. They will provide for preaching, but their first thought will be to create an atmosphere in which people will find it easy to experience the presence of God.

At this point Catholic and Protestant churches differ in their functions. Catholic churches are designed for both private devotions and public worship. During the week and particularly in business districts the faithful come to say their prayers. For this purpose there is a variety of altars as well as the stations of the cross. Protestants for the most part do their personal praying at home, or out under the stars, rather than going to church—although the last-mentioned is increasing. But Protestant churches are designed for common worship, for the people together seeking the divine presence. At its best Protestant worship is a corporate act, with the emphasis upon togetherness.

An architect friend says that his ambition is to build churches where people will instinctively throw away their cigarettes, take off their hats, and hush up. This is good, but not quite enough. A church should so draw men together, one with another, that as a group they may find God. The building itself should be a unifying force.

A wise man has said that a church should first relax a person, and then excite him. It should put us at ease and then inspire us. We shall postpone our discussion of the first of these requirements and consider first how a church can move men's hearts through its very structure.

If a room is to draw people together, it must have a minimum of distractions and a maximum of unity. Neither the eye nor the mind should be drawn hither and thither; both should be directed toward a common goal. This is inherent in the Protestant conception of worship as a social experience.

In the past the unifying element in the Protestant church has been the voice of the minister. At its best, preaching can draw men together and create a spirit which will spread from one heart to another. Few ministers are able to accomplish this from week to week; many can rarely if ever attain it. Preaching is a means of grace and can be a great educational force. Yet every public speaker knows that different people hear different things and that speech does not necessarily unite men. It has a place in worship but it should not be the only or even the chief force in bringing men to God.

Music also has its place in building this spiritual unity. Its contribution to worship will be gone into later.

Most people see far more than they hear. Particularly

with simple people, it is the scene about them that sets the pattern of their thoughts. All of us are the product of our environment to a much greater degree than we will usually admit.

How may a church make the most effective visible impact upon those who gather within its walls? By concentrating the attention of the people upon symbols which will express for them the meaning of their faith. Of these, two are preeminent: the Lord's table and the cross.

Our present thought is that the church is primarily a fellowship of those who are united in the spirit of Christ and dedicated to his service. This fellowship had its earthly climax around the table of our Lord in the Upper Room on the night on which he was betrayed. Down through the ages those who call themselves Christians have gathered about this table. It stands at the center of the worship of the Protestant, Roman Catholic, and Eastern Orthodox branches of the Christian faith. In one form or another the Lord's Supper is both the most common and the most impressive religious observance practiced by men. Most of us have been closer to God in the communion service than at any other time.

On this point the trend in the Roman Catholic Church is significant. Some years ago the high altar in St. Patrick's Cathedral in New York City was removed, and a simple marble table introduced in its stead. The newer churches are generally following this pattern. In some instances the table is being placed in the middle of the room with the people seated about it on three or four sides. The purpose is to get the people close to the table so that they may have a keener sense of participation in the Mass.

The cross is almost inevitably associated with the table. It represents both the death and the resurrection of Christ. It is the universally recognized symbol of our faith. Ever since Calvary it has spoken with power to the hearts of those who would follow our Lord. Therefore a sound instinct is leading an increasing number of Protestant churches to place the communion table and the cross at the center of their worship.

In practical terms, how may this be done most effectively?

Esthetically speaking, the table and the cross are the highlight, the accent, the center of attention of the church. Emotionally, they are what speak to our minds and hearts. For these reasons they should have the utmost distinction. Here is the place for the excitement which the church service should evoke. Here is the spot for strong contrasts.

At this point the first principle is one which is unheeded more often than not. Neither the table nor the cross should match anything else in the room in either color or texture. The best way to muffle the impact of the table is to surround it with wainscoting and furniture of a similar color and grain. In such a setting the table is lost. Similarly treated, the cross fades into the background. Further, the table of our Lord should not be a part of a set, nor should it be bought out of a catalog. Mass production at this point is close to blasphemy. Each church should have a table which is indubitably its own, either designed by the architect for the spot where it is to stand or the work of some craftsman who has created it as a labor of love. If the background is dark, the table should be light; if the surroundings are light, the table may be dark. A marble table can be most striking.

The table of our Lord should be of generous proportions. His supper should not be stacked, but spread. Nothing is more unseemly than the attempt to serve the communion from a tucked-up little table. Of course its dimensions must be in scale with its surroundings, but in new churches the scale should be set by the table. Five feet is a good length, two feet a good width. We believe that it should be a table and not a shelf, with 30 inches a proper height. It should be movable.

The simpler the table, the better. For this reason a solid front is to be preferred to legs. Some panelling may be in order, but complicated designs and lettering are a distraction. A communion table should not need a label. Its position should proclaim what it is beyond the shadow of a doubt. It should not be elaborately dressed but should avoid the fussy or the boudoirish.

The attention of the worshipers has been further drawn to the table and the cross in three ways.

The oldest of these is the reredos, which is a background of carved wood in which there may be a hanging, often changed with the seasons. The reredos is usually in a neutral tone which will not clash with any of the liturgical colors. It can be quite beautiful, but to be appreciated it needs to be seen close at hand. It is expensive—and therefore too often is allowed to swallow up the table and the cross which it should emphasize.

In non-liturgical churches, the dossal is the most

common way of attracting the eye to the table and the cross. This is a hanging in velvet or velour. Like the table and the cross, and for the same reasons, it should not match anything else in the room, but should be quite distinctive. Other things permitting, scarlet is the best color, because it is the most compelling. Anything dull or drab should be avoided. The dossal should be eye-catching. Its proportions should depend upon its surroundings. In any case it should extend six inches beyond the table on either side, so that it will not look skimped from any angle. If it is desirable to accentuate the height of the room, the dossal should be high for its width, there should be deep folds in the cloth, and a panelled effect can be introduced by using braid somewhat in from either edge. Usually the cloth should be 50 percent wider than the area it is expected to fill so as to allow for the folds. These should not be too mechanical or exact. If it is desired to diminish the seeming height of the room, the dossal should be low for its width and should have a strong valance or cornice across the top, with less emphasis on the folds. Unless the dossal is unusually large it should be in a plain color, as a design tends to swallow up the cross. Usually the best place to purchase a dossal is through a department store or upholsterer.

Recently, churches have been built in which the back wall serves as a setting for the table and the cross. This is in contrasting color to the side walls. A slight recess may admit natural light to the central area. The cross is large and of wood and centrally placed on the rear wall. This may be a bit stark, but it is most dramatic. We believe this practice will increase.

Theodore Criley, Architect

Photograph by Julius Shulman

This dramatic façade speaks to the imagination of all comers, while the doors provoke curiosity and invite entrance. The Claremont Church, 235 West Fifth Street, Claremont, California.

Alden B. Dow, Architect

Photograph by Bill Hedrich, Hedrich-Blessing

The altar, the choir, and a profusion of plants are dramatically highlighted by the sun shining through a skylight. First Methodist Church, 114 Jerome Street, Midland, Michigan.

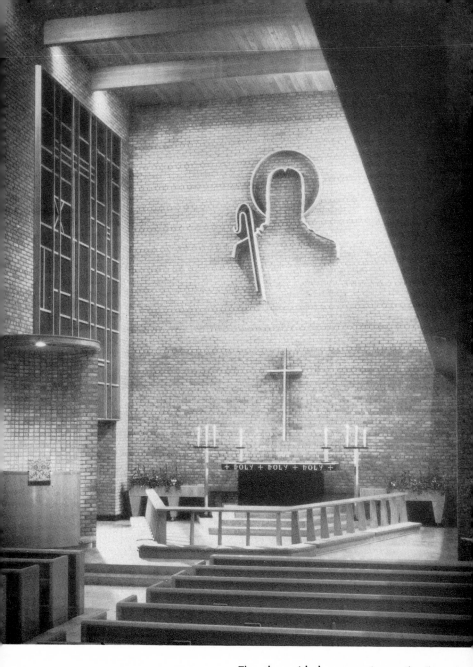

ON THE ALTAR: *+ HOLY + HOLY + HOLY +*

Hills, Gilbertson, and Hayes, Architects

Photograph by Clark Dean, Infinity, Inc.

The three-sided communion rail, the altar and the cross all direct the eye to the stylized silhouette of the Good Shepherd. The Lutheran Church of the Good Shepherd, 4201 France Avenue South, Minneapolis, Minnesota.

Thorshov and Cerny, Architects

This great cross proclaims a house of worship in an unconventional but striking fashion. Fortunate, indeed, are the children of this congregation, for their church faces a city park. The First Christian Church, 2201 First Avenue South, Minneapolis, Minnesota.

Arland A. Dirlam, Architect

Photograph by Paul S. Davis

An off-center cross above an illuminated baptistry holds the center of attention and worship. Lynnfield Street Baptist Church, Lynn, Massachusetts.

Thorshov and Cerny, Architects

Photograph by George Miles Ryan Studios

Natural light and greenery are used effectively to temper the austerity of straight lines and flat surfaces in the interior of First Christian Church, Minneapolis.

William H. van Benschoten, Architect

Photograph by Photo Workshop

A colony of artists helped in the design and decoration of this unusual church, which has translucent panels across the front. This picture was taken at night with both internal and external lighting. St. Gregory's Episcopal Church, Woodstock, New York.

Carr and Cunningham, Architects

Photograph by R. Marvin Wilson, Studio House

The low lines of the educational wing, right, and the church lounge, left, give scale to the central worship area with its lofty spire at the First Congregational Church, Kent, Ohio.

Durham, Anderson and Freed, Architects

Photograph by Kenneth S. Brown

Masonry and wood combine with a metallic spire on a multi-level site, with parking lot adjoining. Fauntleroy Congregational Church, Seattle, Washington.

The materials and size of the cross should be determined by where it is to be placed. There are those who claim that the cross should always have its roots in the earth and therefore should stand upon something rather than be suspended. Apparently the Roman Catholic Church does not accept this position, as it is using many suspended crosses.

In the use of the cross the fundamental principle is that it should be central and dominant, or should not be used at all. It should be treated like our national emblem, the flag. The law forbids the use of the flag in connection with advertising of any kind; custom discourages the sticking of little flags here and there as ornaments. The armed forces insist that the national emblem be treated with respect at all times. The same deference should be given the cross. It should never be used for decoration. We know of churches in which seventeen crosses or more have been carved in the woodwork. This is wrong. If a cross is to be placed upon the communion table, the top of the cross should be above everything else on the table. Too often churches have small crosses and big candlesticks. Sometimes the flowers overshadow the symbol of our faith. There should be but one cross in a church, and that one should occupy a place of undisputed honor.

As for the materials of which a cross may be made, we can find no Scriptural basis for brass, nor do we think that having matching candlesticks and vases adds anything to the cross. Brass does reflect light, and it contrasts well with red, blue, and green, but should not be used with yellow or brown. We believe that brass crosses have been greatly overdone. The original cross was of wood, and it is well to follow this precedent. The most impressive crosses we have seen are of either a light colored metal or of wood. Sometimes decorations add to a cross, but more often they detract from it. Of course there is a place for a wide variety of texture, color, and size, but the emphasis should be on simplicity.

The cross belongs at the focal center of a church. How high this is depends upon the size of the room, but it is usually two or more feet above the top of the communion table. If the room is small, it is possible to put a standing cross on a pedestal which will raise it to the proper level. If the room is large, the cross had better be suspended against either the dossal or the back wall. It should be at the spot where the eyes of the people naturally rest.

Often a shallow shelf, known either as a retable or a gradine, is built just behind and a few inches above the communion table or altar. This provides for the cross, candles, and flowers a place that does not interfere with the observance of the communion, and thus offers one solution to the problem of what to do with the cross at that time.

The drawback to this is that the retable adds a second horizontal line to the one made by the top of the communion table, thereby diminishing the table's pre-eminence and distracting attention from it. High church and low church agree in placing the emphasis on the surface of the table from which our Lord's Supper is served.

Closer to the ideal solution is to have a suspended cross above the table, and to remove the candles and flowers entirely when communion is served. For simplicity, beauty, and spiritual significance the free-standing table is unexcelled.

The other objects commonly placed on or about the communion table are the offering plates and the open Bible, as well as the candles and flowers already mentioned. We shall discuss them in this order.

The offering plates are a useful feature of church life and can be beautiful. However, they should not be kept regularly on the table of our Lord. This is no place for empty receptacles. Only when they are well filled and properly dedicated should the offering plates appear on the table.

In the liturgical churches a missal is kept on a stand on the altar for the use of the officiating clergyman. Some non-liturgical churches place an open Bible in front of the cross. Bibles were never intended to be looked at and worshiped, but to be read. The place from which the Bible should be read is either the lectern or the pulpit. That is where it belongs.

Candles on the communion table are almost inevitable. There is little theory behind this practice. People undoubtedly like the looks of candles, and the burning taper in church seems to speak to something inside of us. A flame is a living thing. It is real and lively and consumes itself. It symbolizes both life and devotion.

Two candles are ordinarily enough. More than this will diffuse too much light, getting into people's eyes. The seven-branched candlestick is a Jewish rather than a Christian symbol. Its use should be restricted to weddings and other brief but festive occasions.

The candles should be subordinate to the cross. If

the cross stands on the table, the tops of new candles should not extend above the cross piece. If the cross is elevated, the candles should be tall, reaching up towards it.

Either the candles should be lit before the first worshiper appears, or the lighting should be the first act in the service. A boy or girl in vestments should come in, light the candles, and then return down the aisle. This suggests that worship is about to begin, and is an excellent way to quiet the congregation.

Flowers also have been brought into the church in response to a deep human sentiment rather than because of any liturgical principle. People love both flowers and the church, so that flowers have become a traditional feature of our worship. In the gloomy churches of the past they brought a patch of light and color. In the austere churches of today the informality of the flowers is a delightful contrast to the straight lines and plain surfaces now in vogue. Both gain from this relationship, as each emphasizes the beauty of the other.

Flowers should not be a mere decoration in a church —something that Mrs. Jones brought in. Nor should they be used to conceal the true character of the building, as is sometimes done for weddings and at Easter, when the motive has often been to overcome some essential ugliness. Flowers should not be a distraction, but should be so related to the communion table and the cross as to enhance their significance. Flowers in church should have a purpose; they should be a part of a composition.

There are those who hold that flowers should never

be placed upon the table of our Lord. Much of the time this is probably a good rule, but we see no reason why the prohibition should be complete. A better rule might be that the flowers should never crowd the table, or the retable. Frequently we find a cross, two candles, and two vases of flowers bumping into each other in a limited space. This is too much. Either the candles or the flowers should be removed.

How the flowers are used should depend upon the position of the cross. If the cross is on the table, the flowers should be on stands on either side. Together with the candles and the cross they should form a pyramid, of which the top of the cross is the peak, and the candles and flowers the sloping sides. The height of the stands should be such as to make this arrangement possible. If communion is not being served and the table is sufficiently elevated, a basket of flowers on the floor in front of the table can also be most effective. If the cross is elevated, the flowers should be placed immediately below it, with the candles on either side.

Different sorts of flowers should be used in different ways. There should be a place for the stiff, high bouquet, and for the low, overflowing one. As the kinds of flowers change, so should their arrangement. For this reason we object to the brass vases, usually memorial gifts, which come as part of an altar set—to which we also are opposed. A church should have a variety of receptacles for flowers, and none of them should be sacred.

One simple rule should govern the furnishings of the communion table. They should form a pleasing composition centering about the cross, which should be the dominant element. If this is kept in mind, varying the arrangements from time to time is most desirable.

Obviously the table and the cross should be completely visible to the entire congregation. Barriers between the congregation and the center of worship should be kept to a minimum.

One of the best ways to draw the eyes of the people to the table is to have a carpet runner in strong color extending from the back of the room to the table. This should not match the dossal but should be rich in texture with just enough pattern so that casual footprints will not show. It will not only help to center the attention of the people, but will give the room greater apparent length and will quiet the footsteps of the congregation, choir, and clergy. Uncovered steps are hurdles which the eye must take, but a carpet eliminates this hindrance. In at least two churches of which we know, the carpet down the center aisle is matched with a dark panel in the ceiling, which also emphasizes depth and directs the eye forward.

The other furniture of the chancel should be so arranged as not to crowd the table or block its view from the pews. How the choir should be disposed will be discussed later. The pulpit and lectern should be placed out far enough on either side to be out of the way of the table. This has two other incidental advantages. When the minister stands at or near the center of the platform he is tempted to swivel as he speaks, directing his attention first to one side of the room and then to the other. When he stands at one side he is almost compelled to take a stance which will include everyone all the time. His voice will usually carry better from this position. At the center the area behind him is "soft," while at the side he is likely to have at his back a hard plastered wall which acts as a sounding board for the voice and lends it resonance.

A special problem is faced by churches in which the congregation comes to the altar rail for the communion. Too often this rail becomes a "fence" that separates the communicants from the table, and obscures their view of it. In new churches the answer is to elevate the altar, so that the platform on which it stands is even with or slightly above the top of the altar rail. Except when the sacrament is served, the rail should be open at the center aisle. Its design should stress horizontal rather than vertical lines.

Churches in some traditions—the Methodist and the Lutheran, to mention two—do not serve continuously, as do many of the liturgical churches, but have the congregation come to the rail in groups, known as "tables," with a separate salutation and blessing for each. In a large church this prolongs the service unduly. A better alternative is to lengthen the rail so that larger numbers can be served at each "table." A good example of this approach may be seen in the Bethel Lutheran Church of Minneapolis, where a free-standing altar is surrounded by a circular rail.

We now come to a question which is usually raised prematurely: What should be the seating capacity of our new church? The answer depends upon the purpose which it is to serve. If it is intended for pulpit oratory and mass evangelism, the carrying power of the preacher's voice is the only limit to the possible size. If the thought is to serve a large, prosperous, powerful congregation which takes pride in its numbers, there should be as many seats as there is reason to believe can be filled.

If the purpose is to provide a place where men may unite their hearts in common worship, the problem is quite different. The question is not how many people can be crowded in but rather what number will derive the most good from the worship. A true congregation is not just a group of people; it is a gathering of men and women who are sharing a common experience. To achieve this the people should be both near the center of worship and close to one another.

This rules out many arrangements which have prevailed in the past. I once preached in a church where the pews formed a great arc. Although there were 90 people present, at no point were they more than three deep! They did not constitute a congregation of worshipers but rather a series of pulpit committees sizing up the preacher. Those who sit in balconies, which are the most expensive seats to provide in a church, are not participants but onlookers. In New England there is usually a dour gentleman sitting over by the windows whose demeanor seems to say, "Preacher, I dare you to tamper with my soul." Those who occupy the back seats are more likely to watch other people pray than to pray themselves. The people who occupy overflow seats on Easter look on, but do not get the deeper meaning of the worship. A church is not doing them much of a favor, or serving its own purposes, by offering casual comers a diluted experience of worship. Few people are won in this way.

Most congregations have an exaggerated notion of

the number of pews which they will need in their new church. One of the cheering signs of the times is that many old churches are so nearly filled that their people resent any suggestion that the seating capacity be reduced. Yet from the point of view of effective worship, keeping down the number of empty pews on ordinary Sundays is more important than providing for the occasional large gathering.

As has been already pointed out, the requirement for corporate worship is that the people be close to one another and near the center of interest. Looking at it practically, eight persons are about as many as can be persuaded to sit in one pew on ordinary Sundays. If there is room for more, they just spread out. To seat eight adults in comfort takes a fifteen-foot pew. Two such pews will give a sideways capacity of sixteen worshipers, which is normally enough. With a five-foot center aisle and two three-foot side aisles this gives a width of 41 feet, which does not require a too-expensive roof span. Under ordinary conditions the effectiveness of the worship diminishes rapidly after the fifteenth pew. Fifteen rows will require a depth of 45 feet and will take care of 240 people. Allowing for 30 or 40 in the choir, and leaving some free space in the rear which can be filled in with chairs, the total seating will be in the neighborhood of 300, with no one more than 60 feet from the communion table. This will take care of most congregations most of the time. It is also an economical size to build as well as easy to maintain.

What if we grow? How about Easter and other special occasions? The answer is to hold multiple services. These have a number of advantages. They permit an economical use of the property, giving a better return on the investment than has been obtained by Protestant churches in the past. They mitigate the parking problem. They make it possible for more people to attend church. The early hours are favored by the parents of small children and by those who want to do something on Sunday besides attending divine worship. A moderate-sized congregation will achieve a greater degree of participation than will a larger one. The minister's message will be taken more seriously. The individual will feel a greater responsibility and a greater sense of fellowship. The entire experience will become more intimate.

Of course there are problems, of which the music is the most obvious. Although there have been choirs which sang for two services, the usual practice is to use two choirs, or possibly a soloist for the early service. Most ministers are glad to preach twice, and will probably do better the second time. It is argued that two services will divide a congregation, with those who attend at one hour not getting to know those who come at another. This should be taken into account in planning the social life of the church on an inclusive basis. However, the larger the congregation, the fewer the social contacts of the individual. Most people will do a better job of enlarging their acquaintance in a group of 200-plus than they will in one of 400. We are almost always better acquainted with the people on our side of the church than with those on the other. It is also true that the people going home from one service often meet the people coming to the other.

In no case has the adding of services hurt the attendance at eleven o'clock to any appreciable degree. We know of two churches which are holding three Sunday morning services, with the later one larger than ever before. Apparently additional opportunities to worship attract additional worshipers. Also, once this custom has become established, it tends to continue. Several new churches adopted the dual service because their quarters were small, but when they moved into a new and much larger building they continued the practice.

The present trend toward corporate worship is giving Protestantism both a new type of church building and a new pattern of church life.

Chapter 7

"CHILDREN OF LIGHT"

In a place of worship, light has both a practical and an inspirational function.

Reading has a part in all forms of Christian worship. The good Catholic follows the Mass in English, while the priest recites it at the altar in Latin. Protestants read the hymns they sing and join in responses and prayers. In every church there is need for enough light so that people with weak eyes can read relatively small type. Often this need is not met.

Light can also stir the human heart. We have always felt that there was much to be said for the sun worshipers. The rising and the setting of the sun are the most inspiring moments of the day. In a church, light can be used to quicken the sense of holy awe which is the heart of worship. Too many churches have given too little thought to the spiritual overtones of light.

Any discussion of light should begin with a consideration of the physiology of the human eye. It can be argued that light exists only as it registers on the eye. No eye, no light!

For our purposes the most significant characteristic of the eye is its truly remarkable power of adaptation. When we are confronted with bright light our pupils contract, our eyelids draw together, and we peek out at the world through an exceedingly narrow slit. In darkness our eyelids open wide, our pupils expand, and in a few moments we can see much.

The essential fact for the builders of churches to remember is that the eye cannot both contract and expand at the same time. This is like trying to walk in two directions at once, and it is painful. Yet this is exactly what happens when we are confronted with an overpowering contrast of light and darkness. We know how blinding an automobile headlight can be. Too often a comparable conflict of a bright light shining into a dark room is found in churches. The eye simply cannot take it.

This situation has often arisen because of the building methods which were necessary in the past. Until relatively recent times the walls of a building were the main support of the roof. To make openings in such a wall was both difficult and hazardous. Safety suggested that windows be few and narrow. Pointed or round tops were used because they weakened the wall less than did square top windows. The result was the lancet window. Its graceful lines were not originally developed in the quest for beauty but rather to provide a safe way to let light into a dark building. It gave a functional solution to a practical problem. Unfortunately the narrow, high window has been continued as the conventional method of lighting churches, long after the necessity for it has passed.

This functional answer inevitably created optical difficulties. On dark days, hole-in-the-wall windows worked fairly well, but when the sun shone through them the sharp contrast between light and darkness was hard on the eyes of the people, particularly when the sun was low on the horizon. Something had to be done to control the intensity of the sunlight. Stained glass was first developed to handle this situation. It did not wholly stop the light, but it did reduce glare. Here, again, the original motive was practical rather than artistic.

Men soon discovered that the glass which mitigated the brilliance of the sun could be most beautiful. Light coming through color often took on a fascinating live-liness. In a day when color was used far less than now this was most welcome. Soon it became traditional that a good church had colored windows.

The origin of stained glass suggests one principle for its use. It is most effective in small windows set in large walls, where it can produce a rich, jewel-like effect. The problems involved in designing a small window are relatively simple. On the other hand, the larger the window, the less the contrast between light and darkness, and the less need there is for controlling the light. Also, the problems of design increase geo-metrically with the area to be filled. Small stained-glass windows are much more satisfying than large ones.

The emotional attachment of church people to stained glass is astonishingly intense. The quickest way the writer could end his usefulness as a consultant in most churches would be to tell the congregation the truth about their windows. A common problem is how to dissuade congregations from building a new church around the atrocious windows which they have come to love in the old church. Viewed in the perspective of the years, this attitude is understandable. Most Protestant churches have been dreary places with little in them to refresh the eyes of the worshipers. The intricacies of the glass offered welcome relief from the boredom of the sermon. It was the one bit of lively color in the place, and became sacred by a process of association.

The lack of the money to pay for them is the prime deterrent to the installation of stained glass in the new churches which are now being built. A frequent practice is to accept clear glass for the windows in the nave but to insist on a stained-glass window in the chancel. Here the danger is that the light shining through the window will get into the eyes of the congregation. At the worst this causes headaches, at the best sleepiness and the inclination to look at the chancel window rather than at the preacher. It is possible for a chancel window to be harmless if it faces the north, is high in the wall, small in size, and the colors are dark blue and greens. Even then it is often a distraction from the communion table below it, which should be the center of interest.

In spite of the objections just stated, churches are still putting in large chancel windows, with or without stained glass. The question then arises, What can we do about it? As far as the window itself is concerned, there is no remedy. Covering the glass with various paints or other mixtures has been tried. These are usually brown or yellow and produce a jaundiced effect to begin with. In the course of time this coating peels off, with curious results. If the window is clear glass, the best answer is to cover it with a hanging and forget about it. If the window is stained glass and presumably a memorial of some sort, the most effective procedure is to equalize so far as possible the light which enters through it, that is, reduce the contrast. This can be done by painting the window-trim and as much of the wall around it as possible white and then directing against the window a battery of floodlights. This will make the situation livable.

The making of stained glass is one of the historic arts which have been developed by the church, and we do not think that it is either likely or desirable that it will become extinct. The better glass makers are doing quite well. Their product has a place even in the so-called "modern" church, but it should be used with understanding and taste. It is particularly fitting in chapels.

Two mistakes mark much of the glass now found in our churches. Our fathers often got too many bright colors too close together, with a garish result. Properly used, as will be pointed out in the next chapter, contrasting colors can be both pleasing and interesting—but should not be jumbled up. They also tried to use glass as a medium for picture making. From necessity a window is a flat surface which must be braced with metal to withstand the pressure of the wind. To do a painting in glass is like the proverbial dog walking on his hind legs; it can be done but it is neither easy nor graceful. The endeavor to get perspective in a medium broken up by strong black lines was particularly unfortunate. The present trend is away from any attempt at naturalism with the pictorial element confined to relatively small medallions and the emphasis on symbolism and the use of rich colors.

The nature of the glass itself has changed. Until a few years ago this was opalescent or "art" glass, in which the variations in color were made a part of the glass itself. This was of uneven thickness, often having ripples, and sometimes used in double layers. Most of the glass now being used is what is known as "antique." It is flat and the color cannot be seen unless it is held up to the light. Variations in color and designs are painted on and then baked in.

Why are the new windows better than the old? is a natural question. The answer is that you can live with them longer. A picture is something that you can look at once, thoroughly comprehend, and then turn away from. The newer windows with their rich symbolism and their subtle interplay of color will hold the attention longer. The contrast is comparable to that between a popular tune which first fascinates and then exasperates, and classical music without words which will bear much more repetition. In our home church I have been looking at some non-pictorial windows for twenty years without becoming weary of them. My only complaint is that the man who did them is dead.

Before ordering stained-glass windows, those who do the selecting need to educate themselves. The newer glass will not make as quick an appeal as will some of the older. One needs to grow into an appreciation of it. A lot of looking needs to be done before any decisions are made. A comforting thought is that the best glass costs little if any more than the not-so-good. The materials and craftsmanship are about the same, while the high-grade designer is in love with his art and less interested in profit than his more commercial competitor. The leading American artist in stained glass, now dead, was accustomed to refer to his firm as "incidentally a business." Dealing with the masters of this craft can be a rich experience.

For most of our readers, stained glass is probably not an immediate concern. The most effective argument for clear glass is its economy. At present it is all that most congregations can afford. One of the significant recent developments is the more effective use of natural light to achieve religious results.

In a church, light should do more than enable people to look about and to read. It can be a means of directing their attention to the proper center of interest. As was pointed out in the preceding chapter, we are building our churches around the communion table and the cross. The light should lead the eyes of the people to these symbols. An effective way to do this is to place the table and the cross against a blank wall on which strong natural light is directed from the side. This was first done by Eliel Saarinen in the Christian Church in Columbus, Indiana, and repeated by him in Christ Lutheran Church in Minneapolis; it has since become common practice. This gives a dramatic center of interest without hurting the eyes of the congregation. The front wall is usually a flat white with a large wooden cross suspended against it.

If the attention of the people is to be focused on the front wall of a church, the side walls should be subordinated to the front. One of the justifications for the use of stained glass has been that it kept the congregation from gazing out the windows. Both of these ends

can be achieved in a variety of ways. The simplest is
to have the windows in the chancel extend to the floor
but to keep those in the body of the church well above
the heads of the people. This gives a bright light at
the front but with a not so bright but adequate illumination in the nave. If these side windows are made continuous they will give the church a strong horizontal
line. A variation of this arrangement is to have windows on one side but not the other, which is desirable
in situations where the sun might be too strong. In
the Zion Lutheran Church of Portland, Oregon, Pietro
Belluschi has achieved a subdued but interesting light
for the body of the church by using random glass
blocks in a variety of colors in the side walls. In the
Village Lutheran Church of Bronxville, New York, and
the Congregational Church in Bellevue, Washington,
the side walls are sawtoothed in such a way that the
congregation cannot see the windows, the light from
which is directed over the shoulders of the people
toward the chancel.

For some unknown reason, reflected light is harder
on the eyes than direct light. Care should be taken to
keep natural light from falling on any highly polished
surfaces. In a church, paint (particularly the "flat"
variety) is much to be preferred to varnish or other
glossy finishes.

The principles which we have been discussing for
natural light are generally applicable to artificial light.
The point which cannot be overstressed is that light
should never shine into the eyes of the people, no
matter what the kind or where it comes from!

Despite the rarity of evening services, artificial light
is becoming increasingly important in our churches.

On dark days and in dark churches it is a necessary supplement to the illumination supplied by the sun. Because of its ever-increasing flexibility, it is being used more and more to achieve religious effects. Light, or the absence of it, can mould the emotional mood of a room.

The lighting practices of today can best be understood against the background of past methods.

For many centuries the only light in the churches was supplied by the sun or by the flickering glimmer of candles and torches. All of the so-called historic styles of church architecture were developed when adequate artificial illumination was unknown. When it is suggested that a church modernize its lighting, a frequent objection is that such a change would be out of keeping with its architecture. The answer is that there is no historic connection between any way of building and any system of lighting. Architecture is old but artificial illumination is very young. When the restoration of the Colonial Church at Lebanon, Connecticut, was undertaken, it was discovered that there was no pattern which could be followed for the lighting—and so the most modern methods were used because they were both the most inconspicuous and the most effective.

Real light first came to the churches through the kerosene lamp and its successor, the gas jet. The illumination thus produced was relatively feeble and did not lend itself to direction. If the people in a church were to see to read their hymnbooks, the lights by which they read had to be nearby. This was achieved by bracket lights along the walls and by low-hanging central chandeliers. About all that could be said for such arrangements was that they made it possible to hold meetings after dark.

Then came electricity. The first bulbs did not carry much further than the gas jets which preceded them, and so they were placed where the lamps or jets had been—and in a few churches they are still there. A common practice was to stud the arches or the balcony front with rows of single bulbs. Over the years the light bulb has become steadily stronger. What was once a mere flicker has become a penetrating glare. This made it necessary to shield the eyes of the people; it also made it possible to remove the source of the light further and further from the pews. This has been done in several ways.

The hanging lantern was the first step, and it is still the most widely used method of lighting churches. The light was subdued by wrapping it up in a combination of heavy glass and metal. Provided too much light did not shine through, the result could be quite pleasing. A lot of current was used up to no good purpose, and only rarely was there adequate light at pew level. Over the years the lanterns have been improved so that they scatter less of their light sideways and direct more of it downward. But even with improvements, hanging lanterns leave much to be desired.

The objections are: first, their initial cost; second, their inefficient use of electricity; and third, the fact that they usually shine in somebody's eyes. When the question is raised with a congregation, the number of people who admit that they are troubled by the lights is amazing. If there is a balcony, the people who sit in it must look through the lights to the front of the church.

The prime argument for hanging lanterns is that people like them. As with stained-glass windows, lanterns have been a colorful addition to what is often a dreary room and have gained a place in the affections of the congregation. This is supported by the contention that they are in themselves beautiful and that they fill in space which would otherwise be bare and empty. Sometimes they form a line which adds to the seeming depth of a church.

If a church wants hanging lanterns, and can afford them, they can be used unobjectionably provided certain rules are followed. There should be no lanterns in the chancel, or over the front pews. These are still being installed in many new churches, but after a Sunday or two they are turned out. Hanging lanterns should be high enough above the pews so that they cannot get in the eyes of the worshipers. With modern directed beam lamps this will not diminish the light perceptibly, and the greater height will permit a wider spread of light, and reduce the number of lanterns needed. Lanterns should never be over the center aisle but to one side, preferably toward the side walls. When a room is over-wide, this will help to draw it together and increase the appearance of depth. The lanterns should be supplemented with other sources of light, such as will be described later. They should be regarded as decoration rather than illumination.

A further step towards getting the glare out of the eyes of the people comes with cove lighting. This is achieved by putting the illuminating element, which is often a tube, around the sides of the room in such a way that it shines against the ceiling. At its best this produces a soft, diffused effect which is relaxing and pleasing to the congregation. If a room is narrow and has a low ceiling it can be illuminated effectively in this way. If it is wide, or the ceiling high, there will be insufficient light at the center. This is probably the most expensive way to light a church because it takes a lot of light on the ceiling to provide adequate light in the pews. It also directs the attention to the ceiling rather than to the center of worship. It will work only with a white ceiling.

Both the hanging lantern and cove lighting are indirect; that is, the light starts in one direction and is then deflected to another. In this process much of its power is lost. We are now finding that this is no longer necessary. Bulbs are available which will direct the light all in one direction and at whatever angle is desired. The conventional lamp of the past cast its light in both a horizontal and a vertical arc—really in the square of 360 degrees. The new bulbs limit their spread to a small fraction of this. They do not scatter light; they concentrate it. This characteristic, combined with their added power, enables them to throw their illumination for surprising distances. The source of the light can be a long ways from the area which it illuminates. Because all the light produced by a lamp arrives where it is wanted, much less current is needed to produce a comparable result than with other systems.

With lights of such power it is obvious that they must be so placed that they will not get into the eyes of the people. Here a simple fact of physics is of great help. Light in itself cannot be seen unless it encounters some substance by which it is reflected. Light is invisible in the interval between where it starts and where it stops. From this it follows that if the source is either concealed or made quite inconspicuous, all that people will see is where the light finally arrives.

The difference between conventional lighting and concealed lighting is like that of facing an automobile headlight or riding behind it. To see the play of light is always pleasing; it is the place of its origin which troubles our eyes.

These new developments have shifted the emphasis in church lighting. Formerly the endeavor was to dress up the places where it started from; now we are getting our results, and also our beautiful effects, from the distribution of the light itself.

The subordination of the source of light is achieved in several ways. The simplest course is to recess the lights in the ceiling. What are known as "down-lights" are barrelled in. They can be adjusted like stereopticon lanterns so that their light will play upon a given area. A simpler arrangement, particularly useful when the light need only travel a short distance, is a recessed box containing a light and possibly a reflector. These are often seen in banks.

Sometimes there is no space between the ceiling and the roof. If there are exposed beams the lights can be placed on the front side in such a way that they cannot be seen except from the front of the church, while their light will come over the shoulders of the people in the pews. If the ceiling is flat, fixtures which will house the lights can be placed against it. If the ceiling slopes and there are no beams, pineapple-shaped lamps with metal sleeves can be hung from the ceiling. With all of these arrangements, the only way one can get glare in the eyes is to stand immediately beneath them and look straight up—which few people will ever do.

Care must be taken in selecting lights of the appropriate angles and so placing them that there will be an even illumination at pew level and no disconcerting shadows on the walls. This is not a difficult problem in adjustment, thanks to the flexibility of the lights themselves.

Here a word of caution is in order. Most of the churches which have installed recessed, directed lamps have gotten twice as much light as they bargained for. Not even the experts seem to realize the difference in intensity of the two systems. When a church finds itself over-lit it can reduce the wattage, turn out half the lights, or just endure it. This may sound cynical, but it is sound economy to take the recommendations of the lighting company or of the salesmen and cut them in two. Most new churches are over-lit.

In addition to general illumination, there are areas in a church to which the attention of the people should be directed at specific times. There should be at least three spotlights at the front of a church—for the communion table, the choir, and the pulpit. The pulpit requires particular attention. If possible, there should be no reading light on the pulpit, because it is almost certain to illuminate the wrong features of the preacher. If he is tall, it may shine upon his breast, or even his stomach. If he is short and it gets in his face, it will eliminate his jaw and play down his eyebrows, giving him a wraith-like appearance. Also, if the spotlight is immediately overhead, it will give the preacher a halo and an exaggerated nose. The correct way is for the spot to play on the minister at an angle of 45 degrees. This will accentuate his eyebrows, play down the nose, and emphasize the jaws. It will also illuminate him well without getting into his eyes. It should be sufficiently strong so that he will not need additional light by which to read.

The atmosphere of a church can be greatly helped by the way the lights are handled. They should not pop on or off—which is one of the objections to fluorescent lights. Rather should the lights in a church follow the example of the sun, and wax and wane gradually. This can be achieved with a rheostat or similar equipment operated by a competent person.

The location of the major light controls is a matter that needs more thought than it generally gets. We have spent weary hours hunting for switch boxes in strange churches. The common idea seems to have been to place them where the boy scouts and idle meddlers cannot find them. Two principles should be followed. The congregation should not be able to observe their operation, but the person who is manipulating the lights should be able to see the results of his efforts. Neither the minister nor the organist should have anything to do with the lights. The controls should be at the rear of the church but so located that the person in charge can *see* which lights are on and which are off. This is far simpler and more foolproof than any system of labelling. Taking care of the lights during the service should be a responsible job for an intelligent layman. It should not be left to chance—or the janitor.

Given modern concealed-source lighting with flexible controls, many lovely effects can be achieved during the course of a service. A ceiling against which no light is directed tends to dissolve into quiet shadows. It gives a church that air of mystery which many people like to associate with religion. As the service progresses the lighting should be varied to suit its various moods. While the congregation is assembling and presumably spending some time in meditation and prayer, the body lights should be at half strength. As the service opens and the people sing, all the lights should be on to express joyousness. When the congregation does not need it to read by, the light should be somewhat reduced in strength. During the anthem the choir lights should be at full strength. During the sermon the spotlight should be on the pulpit and all the other lights dimmed. For the communion service there should be a strong light on the communion table, with only moderate light in the remainder of the church. If these changes are made skillfully, few will notice them. They will not be theatrical, but they will help the congregation to follow the service more attentively and heartily. Special occasions can be celebrated in special ways. Good church lighting properly handled can be a means of grace.

The principles which we have been discussing are strikingly illustrated by four churches which have unusual lighting.

The entire front of the Fauntleroy Congregational Church of Seattle, Washington, is of glass. At first thought it would seem that this would violate our principle that the congregation should not face a strong source of light. However, this circumstance is saved by another principle: that the eye can adjust to almost any degree of brightness if the light is evenly distributed. Three other factors help the situation. The congregation looks towards the north, a grove of trees absorbs much of the glare, and, too, in the wet climate of Seattle the sun is such a casual visitor that its rays are unusually welcome when they are available. The symbolism is that of a church fearlessly facing the world and its problems.

The exact opposite is found in St. Clement's Episcopal Church in Alexandria, Virginia, which has no outside windows whatever. The thought is that the church stands over against the world, perhaps as something of a refuge from it. The church is lit by pinpoints of light in a 14-foot ceiling which appears to be black. The effect is that of the stars on a moonless night. What is really a low ceiling has a suggestion of infinity about it. Although the church seems dark, one can read easily even in a half light. There is more light than there seems to be because it cannot be seen in transit from the little holes in the ceiling to the pews.

To this the Church of the Heavenly Rest (Episcopal) in New York City is in striking contrast. It has no overhead lights whatever in the body of the church. The chancel is lit independently, and there are lights shining up from the floor on the gray stone pillars of the nave, but the working lights are all together on the rear wall of the church, somewhat like those used in a ball park for a night game. This light comes over the shoulder of the congregation at the right angle for reading. When there is any occasion to use either the prayer book or the hymnbook they are on; at other times they are largely off. The worshiper is not conscious of the lights, as they are there when he needs them, and he does not notice their absence at other times.

Riverside Church offers yet another contrast. Although there are hanging lanterns for decorative purposes, the real illumination comes from the high ceiling. This is particularly effective in the chancel, which can be bathed in light. Those who think that the ceiling in their church is too high for recessed lighting should come and see.

A negative lesson is also offered by Riverside. The size of the windows in the tower was set by the Gothic nature of the exterior. The result is that bright sunshine may come through a small window into a relatively dark room, with painful results.

Light can help to get people into a church building. People are like bugs in that they tend to go where the lights are brightest, while we instinctively turn away from anything dark and gloomy. At night, light should point a pathway into a church. The walk leading to the door should be lit up. If there are steps, they should be bathed in light, while the entrance hall should glow with the cheer that only good illumination can bring. And yet how rarely is this done! In most strange churches I struggle with a great impulse to turn on the lights. You never saw a dark entrance to a movie house. A church should sparkle with light.

Protestantism makes much of sociability. Whatever the occasion, those who enter a church like to be both recognized and remembered. The ease with which this can be done depends upon the lighting. Did you ever try to identify someone who was silhouetted against a strong light? You may be able to tell him by his stance, but his features will be lost in a blur. Or did you ever try to get acquainted in a room lit by bridge lamps? Or bracket lights along the wall? Lighting can do much for the friendliness of a church. In those areas where people meet and mingle—narthex, corridors, parlors—the light should be diffused in such a way that no one can get into a shadow. This can best be achieved with fixtures which are recessed in the ceiling or flush against it but that have a wide spread. Notice how the better hotels help their clerks to identify their arriving guests.

In a dining room the problem is similar. If possible the light should fall on the linen-covered tables and then shed a friendly glow on those who are eating. It always helps to really see the food.

The working areas should have the brightest direct light. The first of these is the kitchen, next perhaps the room in which the women sew. Where church school classes do notebook work around tables there should be a strong overhead light.

Any tendency toward uniform lighting should be regarded with strong suspicion. We know of an instance where the local fixture dealer went around with a light meter and then put in exposed lights to give the correct intensity. The result was horrible. The wiser approach is to vary the amount and intensity of the illumination with the uses to which rooms are put. The greater the variety of fixtures used, the more closely can the light be adapted to the needs which it should meet.

Chapter 8

COLOR SPEAKS

LIGHT and color are two phases of the same thing. Color is really nothing more than light broken up into its component parts. Most of the principles covering light hold for color also. The differences can be suggested by thinking of color as a detailed edition of light.

In a church they serve much the same purposes. They can lull a congregation into the mood of repose; they can also stir the hearts of the people. Both are a means by which the attention of the worshipers can be directed.

The emotional appeal of color is more varied than that of light. The sun awakens us and in so doing ignites the fires of hope. The departure of the sun brings repose, and also gloom. Color has a larger vocabulary. Red clamors for attention, suggesting action, danger, sacrifice. Green is nature's favorite, and is generally regarded as inspiring repose. Blue reflects the vastness of the sky, which is often interpreted as impersonal and cold. Yellow is the color of the flickering flame and of gold.

Colors have a way of becoming personal and emotional. We have the "blues," we "see red," the greenish yellows are regarded as sickly hues. In addition, many of us have personal associations with certain colors which may be either happy or unhappy, and which are the reason we like some colors much more than others. The way a church is decorated may affect different people in different ways. This may be an argument for having different types of churches available for different people, or for the same people at different times.

We have seen that the immediate juxtaposition of bright light and deep darkness is painful to the human eye. We do not suffer so sharply from strong color contrasts, and yet they should be used with discretion. Our fathers sometimes got too many brilliant colors too close together, particularly in church windows and organ pipes. The result was garish and oftentimes irritating. On the other hand, a vivid contrast can be positively refreshing, provided that it is in the right place and that there is not too much of it.

Colors are never absolutes. What we see depends only in part upon the chemical composition of the pigments used. The impression made upon the eye is always modified by the intensity of the light and the other colors which may be about. In a church the lights should be installed before any colors are chosen. In redecorating, the first step should usually be to get new lights. The only place where the colors to be used in a room should be selected is in that room itself—and they should be tested by three degrees of light: full daylight, dusk, and artificial light.

Short cuts in this area are dangerous. A large new

church had in its membership an expert on the use of color in advertising, and the congregation undertook to avail itself of his talents. He fixed up a greenish gray color card at home, forgetting that all of the windows had amber glass. When the walls were painted, the yellow light cancelled the green in the paint, and the result was pure mud. The job had to be done over again.

It is not an accident that the spectrum breaks up into a number of colors. We need them, and we should use them. No matter how lovely a color, after a time it becomes wearisome. Figuratively speaking, we need several buckets of paint with which to do a church. Different rooms and areas serve different purposes and should be done in different ways. In certain parts of a church we want to be impressive, in others cozy. Usually there is a place for both comfort and austerity—and each can help the other to be more effective.

Before maple syrup became priceless, a delightful custom prevailed in rural Vermont. The casual visitor was given a saucer full of syrup—and a pickle. After you had consumed the syrup you ate the pickle, and then they refilled your saucer and started over again.

This principle of sharp contrast holds for the decoration of churches. In the past there has been too much matching of woodwork, too little variety on the walls, and often a great lack of imagination.

The experts tell us that basically there are only three color schemes. The first is two tones of the same color, such as light blue and dark blue. The second is two colors close together on the spectrum, such as blue and green. The third is two colors close together plus one from the opposite side of the spectrum for contrast, such as blue and green with a splash of red for liveliness.

In a church there is room for all three schemes. In most corridors and some other areas the sole aim is to be relaxing. This calls for two tones of the same color, such as blue and blue-gray, yellow and buff. Other spots call for a cordial sort of intimacy and the colors used should be brighter and a bit more in contrast, such as a strong green and a pastel turquoise. In the church itself we want dignity and drama, and this calls for a three-color scheme of decoration.

Here another principle comes into play. Dark colors come towards us, light colors move away from us. Provided that there is an abundance of light, strong, vigorous colors can wrap themselves around us. On the other hand, light colors make the rooms in which they are used seem much larger than would otherwise be the case.

Yet another principle is that of balance. Some rooms should be lighter or darker than others, and yet no room should be wholly light or wholly dark. A room that is all white is highly irritating and quite uncomfortable. A room done solely in a variety of browns will be gloomy and soporific. A dash of color in an overly light room will make it much more livable. When a woman has a white kitchen she is likely to keep the sugar in a red can. In a dark room a touch of lively color is like a breath of fresh air. A certain amount of contrast always helps.

Now we are ready to apply these various principles to the specific problem of a place of worship. To repeat, the function of a church is both to relax and to inspire. It should both recognize the individual and impress him.

The color scheme of a church should begin with the front wall. Optically, this should be as far away as possible. A church should look big. Actually the human eye has been developed for discerning distant objects. Only in very recent years have most people done what might be called close work. We are more at ease looking away than watching something close at hand. "I will lift up mine eyes unto the hills" is a natural expression of religious faith. For these reasons the eye of the worshiper should be focused on as distant a point as possible, which is the back wall. This should be the lightest, brightest surface in the room, the nearer chalk white the better.

But this is also the center of the drama of worship, as has been pointed out elsewhere. The eyes of the people should normally rest on the communion table and the cross. Here is where we need our maximum contrast. Here the picture should have its highlight, its accent, to use an artistic term. This can be done in either of two ways. Against the white wall can be placed a large, dark wooden cross which will dominate the church, and beneath it an ample communion table. This arrangement is being used increasingly. The more conventional method is to place a hanging behind the table to draw the eye to both the table and the cross. The cross can be either on the table or suspended above it. If this is done the hanging, known as the dossal, should be the brightest color in the church. Neither it, the communion table, nor the cross should match anything else in the room. Provided that there is no other red in the room, scarlet—the brighter the better—is the best color for a dossal. If the pews are mahogany or there are red carpets and window drapes, the dossal should be green or blue.

In the liturgical churches that change their hangings with the season, the front of the church must be a neutral—white, gray, buff—in order to harmonize with any liturgical color. The necessity of changing the colors on the altar restricts the other walls to light pastels.

The treatment of the front wall controls what is done in other parts of the church. If it is white or near white, great freedom can be exercised in these other matters. If there is a scarlet dossal, the carpet, pews, window drapes must be of a contrasting color.

We have already discussed ceilings to some extent under Light. If the roof is low, it may be desirable to make the ceiling white and give it good illumination. This will have the effect of heightening it. The higher the ceiling the darker it should be, and the less light should play on it. The natural color for a ceiling is that of the sky—blue. A medium ceiling can be a baby blue, a high ceiling midnight blue.

This leaves the side wall. How deep a color this should be depends upon the effect which is desired and the amount of light striking this area. The apparent depth of a room with a light front wall can be greatly increased by darkening the side walls. This also increases the sense of warmth and intimacy. A real color, rather than gray or buff, will add liveliness to the room.

The rear of a church is where people receive their first impression and where they linger to visit afterwards. The atmosphere should be friendly, especially if the social area is in the church itself rather than the entryway. Plenty of free space is desirable with an abundance of light, lots of warm color, and some suggestions of informality. If there is room, an easy chair or two is psychologically helpful.

Many people love a white interior in a church. Properly handled, it is excellent, but certain factors need to be borne in mind. Just painting everything white will not be satisfactory. As we have stressed, the eye becomes uncomfortable when it gets too much light—and white is really embalmed light. The answer is to balance the white surfaces in a variety of ways. If the trim is kept white, a light pastel on the walls will not detract from its glory but will give the congregation greater eye comfort. They may not even notice the difference, but they will feel better. Other ways of balancing the white surfaces is through the use of deep colors in the dossal—which a white church rather needs—the carpets, the drapes at the windows, and the trim of the pews. This will offset the austerity of the white with warmth.

The question is frequently raised as to the effort and expense required to keep a white interior white. The significant fact is that this question is raised by the churches which are not white, while I have never had any strong complaints from the churches that are. Janitors are usually over-burdened and pessimistic souls. We questioned one who had charge of a large church with light pews. He had no complaints. "I have to dust anyway," he explained, "and when I come to some dirt I just rub a bit harder." Even children will respect a white interior and be rather more careful of where they put their feet. And then a little work produces a visible result, which is encouraging, while too many churches look dirty even when they are clean.

The use of plaster for the interior walls of new churches is declining. In its place we are getting bare cinder block or even brick. This is economy, it is also functional, and it gives a church a vigorous touch of austerity which is in happy contrast to the over-decoration and fussy interiors of the past. These surfaces can be painted, and can follow the principles already stated. But this is not necessary. A well-laid block or brick wall can be left unadorned and can be most attractive. The variations in color of the blocks or the brick may give a more interesting surface than a plastered or painted wall, especially if exposed to natural light. Cinder blocks and common brick range in color from light gray to medium brown and are restful to the eye. However, against this background there needs to be strong color somewhere in the room. This can be in the front of the church, in a brilliant dossal, drapes at the windows, or even stained glass. A gray wall sets off bright colors beautifully. We are getting a few interiors with red brick or other dark materials. These call for an abundance of light and for light pews and other furniture. In the churches of the future the structural elements and materials will be far less dressed up than they have been in the past.

This brings us to a word of warning. Our places of worship are large rooms subject to a considerable variation in the lighting of the various parts. Because of these conditions, moderate contrasts in color just do not work out. We once recommended that the chancel of a church be of the same color as the body of the church, only lighter; but the difference did not show and we failed to get the contrast which we desired. A large New England church selected a bright red for the dossal and a darker red for the drapes at the windows, but when the dossal was hung the shadow of the folds darkened the dossal until it appeared to match the drapes. In a church, contrasts should usually be vigorous and unmistakable. We should not hesitate to use color with abandon.

To this general rule there are two exceptions. In a small church or a chapel where the walls and the people are close together, more intricate decorations with fine gradations in color can be used successfully. In a predominantly white church light pastels can produce subtle effects of which the congregation may not be conscious—as we have already suggested.

Color is our greatest aid in correcting the faults in old churches, or even new ones. The working principle is that dark surfaces come towards us while light surfaces move away from us, as we have previously stated. With this can be combined another rule of optics: the human eye travels along the strongest and most dominant lines in a room. These principles can be applied in such ways as to produce surprising results, particularly in changing the apparent proportions of a room.

Many of our old churches appear to be barny because of the excessive height of their ceilings. This situation can usually be remedied without changing the actual height of the interior walls. Simply darkening the ceiling will do much. For this it is usually necessary to recess the lights into the ceiling, to further direct attention away from it. Stressing horizontal lines also helps. If there is a dossal it should be low in proportion to its height and should have a strong cornice or valance across the top. If there are drapes at the windows they should be treated in the same way.

Occasionally a ceiling is too low; and in the future, economy may keep down the height of our new churches. A sense of height can be achieved by reversing the principles stated above. The ceiling should be white, and light should be directed against it. A dossal that is high for its width and that is of two colors or is panelled by the use of braid to divide it into sections, will push up the ceilings. The drapes should be narrow and at the sides of the windows only. All upright lines should be stressed.

The over-wide church is a frequent inheritance from the past. Here the introduction of a center aisle can work wonders, and is usually far less difficult and expensive than is assumed. Even curved pews can be re-cut and re-set without too much trouble. The people love a center aisle for processionals, the bringing forward of the offering, and for weddings. By placing the pulpit on one side and the communion table against the back wall, and laying a runner in strong color from the table to the entrance, the apparent depth of a church can often be doubled. Sometimes the runner can be matched with a panel in the ceiling in contrasting color which will also help to lead the eyes of the worshipers to the communion table. Lightening the front wall and darkening the side walls will also help to change the axis of a church. Hanging lights at the sides may be used to reinforce this front-to-back emphasis.

We suspect that the popularity of the long, narrow church is passing and that in the future one of our problems will be to widen out these shotgun, barrel-like churches. This can be done by reversing the suggestions of the preceding paragraph: by putting more color on the front wall and lightening the side walls. Painting the window frames and sashes either white or the color of the surrounding surface will push them out —and also make them appear larger and give whatever beauty they may have more of a chance.

Flowers and other forms of greenery can be of great help in achieving the effects which we have been discussing. In a church they have two virtues—they are colorful and informal. Nature is never stiff and always friendly. Flowers at the entrance to a church are a most effective way of extending a welcome to all comers. They can also help to draw the eye towards the center of worship.

With larger windows and continuous heat, growing plants are finding an increasing place in the House of God. A janitor with a green thumb or some consecrated soul who loves all growing things can be a great blessing to any congregation.

The function of plants in a church is to break up rigid lines and offset any atmosphere of austerity. In the ornate churches of the past they might add to the clutter, but in the more simple structures of today greenery can refresh the eye and uplift the spirit. Here is color in its original and most natural form. This is particularly needed in churches with brick or cinder block interiors. A climbing vine can redeem a flat surface, while a fern can take the stiffness out of a straight line. Here is where the future will see a great development.

How should a congregation go about deciding what colors are to be used in a church, and where?

From one of our Western states comes a vivid illustration of how not to proceed. Part of the congregation wanted blue, part wanted green, and a few favored some yellow—so they worked out a scheme with equal parts of blue, green and yellow. The church across the street observed the sickly result, and sent for the writer!

At this point the people who profess to have "good taste"—whatever that is—are to be distrusted. Just to be pretty is not enough for a church. Nor should the person who says, "My wife picked a nice green for our dining room; wouldn't that be nice for the church?" be given much attention. In a church every color should have a purpose both in itself and in its relation to other colors. The first step should be to define what it is that you are trying to do. Where do you want to put people at ease? Where is the place for a cordial sort of intimacy? Where should a church be frankly impressive? When decisions have been reached on these points, the principles which have been outlined in this chapter will show you how to attain the effects that you have in mind.

If the ends to be achieved are defined and the laws of color are understood, almost any group of ordinary intelligence can work out a satisfactory color scheme for a church. This will work better than turning the job over to an interior decorator. These people know more about color than they do about churches. They are likely to think up a chromatic theme song and apply it to the entire setting. We know a church where the most striking use of color is in the really gorgeous fabric used to upholster the seats of the pulpit chairs. This is beautiful and possibly artistic but also quite out of place. If an interior decorator is available he may be most helpful in selecting specific colors after the general purpose has been worked out. Yet we know of an instance when a dozen men working with the local paperhanger and his book of colors developed a scheme which has proven most satisfactory. As with the other problems involved in building a church, the more thinking someone does before decisions are made, the better. Too often the responsible parties are suffering from brain fag when the time comes to consider the right use of color.

Nearly every week I drive through the countryside on my way to preach in some church. Nature is always interesting and often radiant. The sky, the earth, all growing things have much sparkle. Usually this ends at the door of the church. Where men gather to worship the God who created this colorful world is too often a room that is commonplace, dull, and drear. The last thing to be found in many churches is sparkle. Let us endeavor to bring into the House of God more of the radiant glory of His world.

Chapter 9

SOUND CONTROL

A PROTESTANT church is traditionally a place of verbal communication. In it people come to listen and to talk. And the effectiveness of the building in which this takes place depends in large measure upon how well it prompts both processes. To judge this, four basic considerations must be taken into account:

1. Moments of complete silence are essential if the congregation is to experience the presence of God in worship.
2. The congregation must be able to hear clearly the words of the minister, as well as the music of the organ and choir, without undue effort.
3. It should be possible for groups ranging in number from six to twenty to talk back and forth with each other comfortably in class sessions and business meetings.
4. Individuals should have no difficulty speaking with each other.

Often it is necessary that two or more of these situations be carried on in the same room.

Sounds are transmitted by vibrations, many of which can pass through seemingly solid materials. Deep notes and staccato sounds are the most penetrating: a bass voice carries further than a soprano, and a piano will be heard at a greater distance than a violin. These are, however, simply differences of degree. All sounds are produced and transmitted in essentially the same fashion.

In a church, sounds can be dealt with in three ways —amplifying it, reducing its volume, and stopping it.

Sounds can be *amplified* so that they will carry farther and be heard more readily. This is done by prolonging the period of vibration of each sound. If there is a hard surface behind the minister, the organ, or the choir, the sounds which they produce will have increased resonance. Speaking or singing out-of-doors is difficult just because this background is missing. To achieve resonance is one of the reasons why churches are built.

The danger is that rooms can easily become too resonant. Too much hard surface, or two hard walls opposite each other can prolong sounds until they run together in a roar. If the two hard surfaces are at a distance from each other, they may produce the same sound twice—an echo, in other words.

Just how long sounds should be prolonged in a church is a difficult question. Bach and the other classic musicians were accustomed to composing music to be performed in stone churches with a high degree of resonance, and their compositions are most satisfyingly heard under such conditions. The older type of oratory, such as that practiced by William Jennings Bryan, was more orotund and deliberate than the public speaking of today, which cultivates an informal, conversational approach. High-fidelity recordings and the wider appreciation of chamber music are two developments accustoming us to hearing more notes more clearly. The contemporary tempo in speech and music is quicker.

Thus, today we find that one second of sound prolongation is sufficient for most speakers; two or three seconds is better for music. A workable compromise which is not too hard on either the preacher or the musicians is one-and-a-half to two seconds.

Another way in which sound can be amplified is with the microphone and loud-speaker. When a church has a seating capacity of more than three hundred, or if the auditorium is cut up by balconies and alcoves, the loud-speaker may be necessary; but it should be a last resort rather than a first step. However, there is often need for mechanical amplification in the other meeting rooms of a church. When public-address systems are used it should be remembered that sound travels faster by wire than by air, and care should be taken to see that the microphone does not pick up and repeat the sounds coming from the speaker. However, amplifying systems do not work themselves. They need constant adjustment and even then may fall into strange ways. They should be used as little as possible. The best way to get good acoustics is to build them into the room.

A second treatment commonly given to sound in a church is *to reduce its volume*. This is done through the use of sound-absorbent materials, which are in general soft and spongy. The most popular and effective materials are acoustical tile and soft plaster. We are all familiar with the white, perforated tiles found on the ceilings of restaurants, banks, and schools. Fiber board with holes in it also picks up sound. Anything which makes these materials less porous diminishes their value as sound absorbers. Only certain paints, specially prepared for this purpose, therefore, should be applied to them.

The oldest and probably the best sound absorbers are animal and vegetable fibers. In a church these are found in carpets, pew cushions, drapes of all sorts, and above all, in the clothes of the congregation. A well-filled church is rarely over-resonant.

However, it is important to remember that materials which seem to absorb sound do not really stop them. They are filters, or sieves, rather than barriers. An acoustical ceiling will quiet the room, but this will not prevent the sounds originating in that room from penetrating into the room above it. A cinder-block partition is an excellent sound-softener for a school room, but it does not prevent the sound from escaping into the next room. Nor do soft materials which reduce vibrations within one room prevent those vibrations from continuing on their way.

This brings us to the third treatment given to sound in a church, which is *to stop it*. This is a difficult undertaking. There are just three ways in which absolute quiet can be achieved in a church. The first and best is the separation of the various rooms in space, as is being done in the campus-style church. Building on one level rather than on several also helps. The second successful barrier to sound is solid masonry—the heavier the better. However, for even more practical reasons, we are using less and less stone and brick in the construction of churches. The third way to stop sound is with two hard surfaces sandwiching an air space or some soft material. This can be done with plaster walls on studs which are staggered, so that there is a continuous air space for the vibrations to jump across. In the past, acoustical "blankets" were woven between the studs, but this practice seems to be declining. If there are doors in such a wall, they should be weather-stripped, or made double with an air space in between.

Now we shall apply these principles to the specific areas found in most churches.

Since the place of worship is the heart of every church, it is the spot where it is vital to have complete silence at times. Fortunately, competing noises from outside are diminishing. Horn blowing is becoming increasingly unpopular; the clanging street car has followed the clomping of horses' hooves into oblivion. The day when churches were ventilated by opening windows is about over. The preacher faces less outside competition.

On the other hand, the practice of having at least some of the church school classes going on at the same time as the church service is increasing. In building new churches it is important that the place of worship be as separate as possible from the areas used by the church school.

Within a place of worship it is desirable to maintain a proper balance between sound-reflecting and sound-absorbing surfaces. If there is too much of the former, the room will roar; if too much of the latter, the music will "go dead," and the preacher will need an amplifier to be heard. In theory an acoustical engineer should be able to write a prescription guaranteeing good acoustics in a new church, but two difficulties arise at this point. The number of competent acoustical engineers is limited (with most of them in Boston) while there is a preponderance of self-styled practitioners of this art who are in reality merely disguised salesmen for acoustical materials. A further complexity is that even bona fide acoustical engineers are not infallible, and occasionally churches which have used their services have run into problems. A good method is to use the best available talent, and then proceed by trial and error, if that becomes necessary, adding hard surfaces if there is need for more sound, or soft surfaces if the room is too noisy. We recently discovered a church with a bit of curving glass behind the pulpit—an excellent means of strengthening the minister's voice. On the other hand, if the acoustics of a church are good, but drapes are needed for decorative purposes, they should be of glass fiber or plastic materials to avoid upsetting the balance of sound. Fortunately, steps such as these are not unduly expensive.

Most churches have a multi-purpose room where church school classes meet, suppers are held, games are played, and the women's society gathers. With many new congregations, the parish hall also serves for the Sunday morning worship. How the room is to be treated acoustically should depend upon the importance attached to the various activities which it must serve. If worship is primary, hard surfaces should be stressed. If the church school lesson period and dinners are stressed, the room should be given the maximum of acoustical treatment, and a public address system installed for the occasional general meetings held there.

Teaching areas gain greatly from the use of sound-absorbent materials. We once found seventeen primary classes in one large room doing surprisingly well, thanks to an acoustical ceiling and a good floor covering. Cotton or woolen drapes also help. If there are to be screens separating classes, their surface should be cotton or wool, or perforated fiber board—and they will help appreciably in keeping down sound. On the other hand, even the most modern folding partitions cannot prevent noises from progressing from one area to another.

Traditionally, Protestants are a friendly, talkative people. A secondary but potent reason for going to church is to visit with one's friends. While noise in the worship area should be avoided, sociability among the congregation should by all means be encouraged. All places where people meet one another in a friendly way should be given the maximum acoustical treatment. This is particularly needful at entryways, on corridors and stairways—usually the noisiest parts of a church. Parlors and offices need carpets, drapes, and sound-absorbing ceilings. The kitchen, noisy by its nature, is a particularly difficult problem. Indeed, deadening the kitchen noise calls for real resourcefulness, since acoustical tile is discouraged by law for fear grease might get into the little holes and create a fire hazard.

To sum up, the time and effort expended in determining and solving the acoustical needs of your church will pay off handsomely in an improved ministry; for, to paraphrase a biblical inquiry, How shall the congregation learn what is required of them as Christians, except they first hear the Word?

Chapter 10

GIVING MUSIC ITS PLACE

IN CREATING the mood of worship, architecture and music are allies. By its appeal to the eye, the place in which worship is held sets the scene and creates conditions which predispose us to feel a sense of awe. Music, speaking to the ear, heightens the mood. The spoken word, building upon these foundations, adds meaning, thus gaining the consent of the mind.

Music is the medium through which Protestants have traditionally expressed their religious emotions. In song we forget ourselves and draw near to God. It is our most active mode of worship.

Church music has two aspects. The most important is that in which the people as a whole participate—the singing of hymns and responses. The second is the singing which the choirs do for the congregation. The difference between the two should be of degree rather than kind. We have choirs because in the past, at least, musical training and skills were restricted to a limited number of people. The church choir is a device by which the few were able to do that which was impossible to the many. At its best, however, the choir always represents the congregation. Its function is vicarious. It does not sing to the people but for them. It is their mouthpiece. Through song it expresses emotions which the congregation feels but to which it cannot give utterance.

The great increase in the popular knowledge and appreciation of music is narrowing the gap between the choir and the congregation. This is apparent in the multiplication in the number of choirs and their growth in membership. The old paid quartette is almost extinct. An increasing number of churches are getting along without any paid singers whatsoever. More and more congregations are accepting the ideal of training the children and young people through graded choirs for service in the principal choir—and then graduating them into the congregation. Ultimately the wall between the two will become exceedingly thin. Let us hope that the Lutheran custom of "singing the service" either with a choir or without, may spread to other denominations. In the meantime churches are facing the problem of providing room for their growing choirs.

Where will we put the choir? is the question which confronts anyone who undertakes to build a church. In the past there have been three answers.

A balcony in the rear of the church was used by early American choirs, and is still the customary place in Roman Catholic churches. Some choirs have continued in the balcony through the years; a few have returned there from other locations.

The argument favoring a balcony choir is that the

congregation cannot see the singers, and that this permits the conductor to lead in a vigorous way and enables the choir to sing without self-consciousness. Also the congregation's attention is not distracted by the choir during the service.

The arguments against the balcony location are that the choir is too far from the people to lead them in the hymns; the singers do not participate in the worship; and they often fall into bad habits, arriving late, leaving early, and indulging in non-religious activities when they are not singing. A processional is difficult with a balcony choir.

The next location was on the platform behind the minister and facing the congregation. This arrangement came in, in most instances, with the installation of an organ. This instrument cost money; those who paid for it wanted to see as well as hear it; consequently it went down in front. The organ helped the choir to sing, and so they took their place in front of it.

The objections to this arrangement are that the choir and congregation staring directly at each other produce mutual self-consciousness and discomfort, which encourages the congregation to flee to the back pews; that in this position the choir's efforts and impact resemble those of a concert more nearly than worship. A further disadvantage is that they can see only the back of the minister. With the current growth in choir size, most choir lofts at the front of the church have become entirely inadequate, while expansion is most difficult if not impossible.

In recent years the "divided chancel," in which the choir sits in two sections facing each other, has enjoyed a great vogue. Nearly all new churches have been built on this pattern, while thousands of old ones have been remodeled to conform with it.

This has been commonly accepted as a return to the practice of the past, but history does not bear out the theory. Prior to the Reformation there were no chancels in the parish churches of England. The custom of two groups sitting opposite each other and singing, often antiphonally, was not developed for congregational worship, but grew up in the monastic and university chapels of the middle ages. Today in Latin lands one can find groups of monks carrying on a service in the portion of a church known as the choir with complete disregard of any possible worshipers or onlookers. In our country this arrangement can be seen in the General Theological Seminary in New York, in the Protestant Episcopal Seminary in Philadelphia, and in St. Paul's School, Concord, N. H. This plan of facing pews was adopted for the edification and inspiration of the participants sitting in them rather than for the benefit of any further congregation.

We suspect that the popularity of the divided chancel in parish churches is due to the way it breaks up the previous staring match between the choir and the congregation. In this country the arrangement is unknown in the Roman Catholic churches, probably because the problem of singers and worshipers facing each other has not arisen with them. It also gives to small churches an increased appearance of depth. The open space it provides for the reception of the offering, processionals, and weddings is appreciated. It is usually an improvement over what preceded it.

Yet there are numerous valid objections to the chancel as the location for the choir.

Musically, a choir does not naturally divide into two sections. This arrangement was originally intended for two choirs. If the organist is seated so that he can see those on one side, he cannot see those on the other side except through a mirror. Musicians—when they dare speak their mind—do not like it. Clarence Dickinson, the dean of American organists, has told me, "The chancel arrangement presents no insuperable difficulties for the choir," which is putting the matter charitably.

Liturgically, it has several objections. If the two divisions of the choir are seated close enough together so that they can sing as a unit, they crowd in upon the communion table, separating it from the congregation and making of the communion a mystery hidden from the eyes of the people. If the two sides are far enough apart so that the people can see the table, their separation makes it difficult for them to sing together. The singers are separated from their fellow worshipers. They have an imperfect view of the preacher and often cannot hear him well. For these reasons the vogue of the chancel is beginning to wane.

Few churches, if any, will ever attain ideal musical arrangements. However, there are certain principles which will help almost any church towards this end.

Because a pipe organ is a large instrument which is difficult and expensive to move, we may well begin with it. In the past, churches have been built without much thought for the organ, particularly if it was not installed until some years later. The mechanism is often tucked away in strange places, such as chambers built onto the church, or up in the attic. It has been hidden behind rows of non-speaking but supposedly impressive pipes. If a congregation is willing to pay what a modern pipe organ costs, the organ should be so located as to be played to the best advantage. The rule is simple: the mechanism of the organ should be in the same room as the people who listen to it, and there should be a minimum of barriers between the speaking pipes and the congregation.

This means that the organ should be planned for when the church is built, and in consultation with a competent organ builder or organ architect, preferably one who has nothing to sell beyond his own services. The plans should be worked on until the organ is located where it can best be heard, which is out in the open. Provided that it does not claim undue attention, we see no reason why the mechanism of the organ needs to be concealed in any way. As a number of churches have discovered, including St. Paul's Episcopal Cathedral in Boston, the natural silver-lead color of the pipes is far more pleasing than the decorations which have been inflicted on them, while the ranks of pipes follow graceful lines and are inherently interesting. With modern controls, sound boxes with their noisy shutters are becoming less necessary. If a church is unwilling to go completely functional, whatever is used to conceal the pipes should be of a sound-transmitting material: glass fiber, plastic, or a fish-net type of fabric. Animal and vegetable materials should be avoided. The objection to both ornamental pipes and heavy grills is that they stop sound.

The organ and choir should be together, so that the

organ may support the voices of the choir and its sound come through the choir to the people. We believe that both should be in the front of the church, but not in such a way as to dominate the scene or compete with the communion table and cross as the center of interest.

Unfortunately, this principle does not hold for the electronic organ. Here the difficulty is that too much sound comes from too small an area, and that anyone who gets in its direct path is bowled over by it. Where to put the sound box is the greatest problem connected with this type of instrument. The answer is twofold. If possible, have two sound boxes and locate them in different portions of the room. Place the outlets of the sound boxes above the heads of the congregation and choir. With this arrangement the ceiling distributes the sound. Since most electronic organs are in small churches, there is no problem of lag.

The next principle holds whether the church has a pipe organ or an electronic instrument. The console should be at a sufficient distance from both the organ mechanism and the choir so that the organist can hear both much as the congregation hears them. When the organist is too close to the source of the music, he is often drowned in his own sound and cannot judge his volume correctly. Separation permits him to modulate the organ so as to achieve the best results.

Often choirs object to being away from the console, but we believe that this is largely psychological. Actually the organist can get a better view of the choir and give such signals as may be necessary, from a distance, than when the singers are right on top of him. Ten feet is the ideal distance.

How can these musical arrangements be fitted into the plan of a church in such a way as to enhance, rather than interfere with, its primary purpose of inspiring the spirit of worship? This can be achieved in several ways.

For a small church it is practical to put the pulpit and the organ console on one side of the platform and the choir on the other, with the organist and the singers facing each other.

In larger churches the choir may be placed on the floor level of the church, in front of the chancel area facing toward the console, which should be on the opposite side. Space can also be provided for a second choir on the console side. In Lutheran and German churches it has been common to place the choir in the transept of the church.

From the point of view of worship, the more the choir is included in the worshiping congregation, the better. They should be thought of simply as a portion of the congregation which has been given certain special duties of leadership. For good congregational singing, the closer the choir is to the people in the pews, both vertically and horizontally, the better. Singing which is near at hand is contagious. One of the great virtues of processionals and recessionals is that they tend to involve the people in the pews in the hymns.

Two additional needs of the modern choir are a place to keep their music and gowns and a place in which to rehearse.

In the past one of the weakest ideas with which architects were plagued was to put the choir room on one side of the chancel or platform and the minister's study on the other. This is the worst possible location for either because this area is generally neither easily accessible, nor large enough. Where the choir robes are kept should be at some distance from the place where the choir sings. A group of people preparing to sing is rarely quiet. Such a group also needs quite a bit of space, even though for only a short period of time. The necessity of going some distance encourages a processional. (It also discourages the tendency of forgetting various items, and going back after them.)

Only the largest churches can afford rooms for robing and nothing else. What the ordinary church needs are closets and cabinets off either a parlor, parish hall, or corridor, where the choir things can be kept and also gotten at easily.

Some churches have elaborate rehearsal rooms, with chairs for the singers arranged in tiers around a grand piano at which the choirmaster sits. The arguments for this are that in the past it has been difficult and expensive to heat the church itself for a rehearsal, and that it is easier for a choir to practice with a piano than with an organ. However, such a room is quite an expense. It is possible that modern insulation and heating, combined with a choir arrangement which puts all the singers in one group, may make the separate rehearsal room somewhat less necessary.

Many, although not all, choirs like to "warm up" on Sunday morning before the service. If good work has been done at rehearsals, we wonder how necessary this is. It creates problems for the church school and sometimes disturbs the assembling congregation. Where to have the "warm-up" is puzzling. In California we found a church with a cabin up in the woods which was used for this purpose. That was perfect. Where there are basements we have sometimes suggested that they might be used for this purpose. Such periods of vocalizing are always short, with everybody standing. What is needed is some degree of isolation. Even though a basement be crude and unsuited to most purposes, it might function well in this capacity.

Music is becoming increasingly important in Protestant churches. The physical facilities which are needed should have far more thought than has been given them in the past. A happy choir and a contented organist are a great asset to any church.

Chapter **11**

THAT THE YOUNG MAY KNOW GOD

As we have pointed out, the birth rate is probably the greatest single stimulus to church building today. Many congregations are more disturbed over the difficulty of finding a place to put the children than about any other factor.

This is more than a matter of too many children and too little space. The conception of what constitutes adequate facilities has changed greatly over the years. One who has known the Sunday schools of other days is astonished at the current interpretation of the adjective "crowded." Complaints are raised at conditions which would once have been accepted as excellent. What this means is that our standards are rising.

Today there is no accepted pattern for the physical accommodations for the church school. The congregation which wants to build has nothing to copy. This is all to the good.

When the teachers are asked what they want, the almost universal answer is separate classrooms. They imagine that if only they could get their children within four stout walls, their troubles would be over. It is not as simple as this. We can show you plenty of classrooms which are ugly, noisy, and terrible places in which to teach. The incompetent teacher will have more trouble in a room by herself than out in the open. However, the church school people will usually come to the building committee with one of two propositions. The more common is to add up the number of classes and say, "Give us this many rooms." A variation is to add the number of children of different ages and take the experts' recommendation of how many square feet a child of a given age should have (with the smallest ones taking up the most room) and then present a grand total of space requirements in square feet. The fallacy in both approaches is that the needs of today will not be those of tomorrow. An institution which ministers to growing children is bound to change. Many of the people who built our present churches thought they had our needs very neatly figured out for us! There is no reason to believe that we can do much better.

A more immediate objection to this so-many-rooms-or-so-much-space approach is that exceedingly few churches can afford to build on that scale today. Usually the churches which have lots of money have relatively few children, while those that are overflowing with young life are often short on cash. With present costs, to build rooms which will be used for only forty minutes a week for about forty weeks out of the year does not make economic sense, even if the money were available.

Provided that we do not regard separate rooms as the only solution to the problem of the church school, the situation is not impossible. What is needed is a sufficient flexibility of mind to try new ways. We encountered one church which was far more ready to raise $100,000 than to change its habits. This is an area where conservatism can be costly.

Behind the demand for separate rooms lies the desire for good teaching conditions. With this aim no one can quarrel—but the two are not necessarily synonymous. The profitable approach to this problem is first to analyze what the physical factors are which make good teaching easy.

At this point something should be said about the change in teaching methods which has taken place. It was once assumed that if the teacher could "tell it to them" in such a fashion that they heard—and presumably understood—then the children would learn. Today we know that it is not this simple. No impression lasts which is not followed by some form of expression. The child should respond in other ways than by just listening. He should do something.

This has led to an increased emphasis upon an abundance of open floor space, particularly for the smaller children. The church school is no longer a place where small boys and girls sit huddled up together on little red chairs. Even the older children move around more than formerly. What is needed is plenty of floor space, but this space does not need to be dedicated wholly to the church school.

A second condition for good teaching is sound-control. With the younger children this is less important than with the older ones. Where one has to shout to be heard, discussion is impossible—and dogmatism is almost inescapable. It is difficult to be tolerant in a loud voice! If teacher and pupil are to talk back and forth, quiet must prevail.

In the endeavor to combine flexibility in the use of space with sound-control during the class period, many churches have installed movable partitions. This has appealed to gadget-lovers, who are always with us. These ingenious contraptions have rarely been satisfactory. Usually they are ugly, difficult to operate, noisy when they do work, and utter failures as far as stopping sound is concerned. Once a movable partition is closed it is almost impossible to get through it without creating a disturbance.

The accordion-type door is a refined edition of the old movable partition. It looks better and works more easily, but its durability is open to question. For psychological separation it is excellent; shutting off the rear of a church when attendance is scant, or reducing the size of a dining room so that a small group will not be lost. The only way that it can effectively control sound is to have two walls with an air space in between. Most churches have found the accordion-type door disappointing as a means of separating classes.

Recent years have brought a new method of sound-control in the use of acoustical plaster or tile, usually on the ceiling. Such treatment has little effect upon sounds which come from without, but it does exercise a remarkable control over the noise which originates within a room. The public schools report that four reading classes can be conducted at the same time in an acoustically treated room without interfering with each other. After installing an acoustical ceiling in a parish hall where a number of classes had been meeting separated by movable screens, the rector of a Rochester, New York, Episcopal church, reports, "We no longer bother to set up the screens." Acoustical tile has transformed many restaurants from a place of din to a spot where it is easy to converse in a normal tone of voice.

Acoustical treatment is often more needed in small rooms than in large ones. Any room where the voice roars should be given attention. Much confusion can be eliminated by the use of acoustical materials in entryways, along corridors, and on stairways. It can be said emphatically that most areas which are used for teaching, regardless of their size, should have such treatment. The teachers' work will thereby be made much easier.

An orderly setting is another prerequisite for good teaching. A disorderly room invites disorderly conduct. Children behave according to the setting in which they find themselves. A minister charged with the supervision of churches had to visit a rural congregation on two successive Sundays. On the first trip he found some boys "tearing the place down" when he arrived. Next week he got there before the boys and placed a cross and two lighted candles at the front of the room—and the disturbers of the peace on the preceding Sunday came in on tiptoe!

Most rooms where church school classes meet need to be uncluttered. A mass of this and that is subtly irritating. Much of it could probably be thrown out, and proper storage facilities should be provided for the rest. Adequate cupboards and closets, effectively used, will work wonders in inducing quiet and seemly behaviour on the part of the children.

For good teaching facilities we have seen that it is necessary to have a proper amount of floor space, good sound control, and sufficient storage facilities to make possible an orderly setting. With this general background we shall now consider the specific needs of particular age groups.

We will begin with the smallest children. For many a church they are both the greatest problem and the biggest opportunity.

In the long view the smallest children are the most important people who attend a church. They will outlive the rest of us. Whatever impression we make upon them will be bearing fruit when we are gone and forgotten. From the point of view of the church, they are prospective long-time customers. A high school boy will soon vanish into college, the army, or a job at a distance. A toddler can be expected to keep on coming for fifteen years. Society is slow discovering that it is the smallest children who really learn the most. When a distraught parent goes to a child psychologist he is usually told, "Your present troubles are due to mistakes which you made some years ago." The formation of a child's character begins at birth. The earlier Christian influences are brought to bear upon a young life, the greater are the chances that they will be dominant. The church cannot start too soon.

The smaller the child, the more likely it is to lead its parents into the church. Birth is the greatest miracle of life and is an essentially religious experience. Most couples are nearer heaven when they look into the eyes of a newborn child than at any other time. The sooner the church moves into the picture effectively, the better.

For this reason we are convinced that next to a place of worship, the accommodations for small children are the most essential facilities for a church. Here is where a liberal investment will pay the largest returns both in lives and in dollars. As we have already pointed out, the little child must be brought to church. If he is there, his parents will be with him. The older a child gets, the less likely is this to be the case. By the time they get to high school young people are prone to go one way and their parents another. The time to claim the parents for the church is when the children are small.

If possible, the place to begin is with a crib room where the smallest babies can be left while their parents attend church.

This should not be confused with what is known, rather unhappily, as the "cry room," which is a sound-proof room at the rear of a church where the mothers can dangle their babies on their knees while they look out at the congregation through a window and listen to the service over a loud-speaker. Given two mothers and two babies in such a room, they will find something much more interesting to do than ponder the words of the preacher. As one preacher's wife put it, "Why should I go to such a place to tend my baby? I can manage him a whole lot better at home!"

What most couples want and need on Sunday morning is to be separated from their darling for an hour so that they can sit shoulder to shoulder in the peace of the House of God and in the company of their fellows. Bringing up a baby is a confining life; moments of escape are highly prized.

Parents will not trust their babies to the care of the church unless they are sure that their little ones will be in competent hands. If at all possible, this should be a professional rather than an amateur venture. We know of a church which pays a nurse five dollars a Sunday to look after the babies, and which figures that it gets its money back on the offering plate, not to mention the new families brought into its fellowship. In another church the trained nurses in the congregation take turns running the crib room. An excellent practice is for married couples to take turns. They will conscientiously attend the babies, while the presence of a man will discourage mothers from lingering. To be avoided in any event are talkative groups of women, and high school girls acting as baby sitters.

Whoever is in charge should be strong-minded if not dictatorial. The purpose should be to return the babies to their parents in as good shape as when they came. To this end no doubtful persons with sniffles or skin troubles should be admitted. Grandparents and other interlopers should be excluded. The mothers themselves should be encouraged to go on to church rather than to sit around and talk with one another.

The first requirement for a crib room is that it should not only be clean but that it should *look* clean. We know of a church where the cribs, play pens, and other furniture are scrubbed down every Saturday.

A crib room should be easily accessible but if possible with a separate outside entrance so that the little folks can be brought and taken away without mingling with the rest of the congregation. In Springfield, Missouri, we discovered the ultimate along this line—an old house with a big sign across the front reading "Baptist Baby Building."

Obviously there should be an abundance of cribs for sleepy babies and play pens for the lively ones, with some high chairs for those in between. A sink is a great convenience. We found one church which had signed up with the diaper service and had a snowy pile of "changes" waiting for next Sunday's business.

Furnishing a crib room is about as popular a project as a church can undertake. Judging by the assortment of furniture, it would appear that in some congregations everyone who has lost hope of another child commonly donates their equipment to the church. To conserve space, one church had double-decker cribs. Such facilities are also used during the week whenever there is a famliy meeting. All in all, the crib room's growing popularity is one of the hopeful signs of the times in Protestantism.

Let us trust that in the future many children will never know when they started to church but will just naturally grow up on the premises. That day is not yet. Most children today must face a "first Sunday." This is really a momentous occasion. If all goes well, another soul may be won for the Kingdom and another family for the church.

But the first Sunday is not always a happy occasion. We were present when a four-year-old in charge of his big brother arrived at a church where the kindergarten meets in the kitchen down in the basement. The new recruit took a look into this gloomy hole and then let out a yowl and refused to go in, which may have been evidence of intelligence. He cried until taken home. At another church the minister's three-year-old was ushered into a large room with 50 children, most of them under eight or nine. He surveyed the situation and then declared in a loud voice, "I want to go home!" In another instance a three-year-old was brought for the first time to a church which had no accommodations other than a kindergarten. The child got along all right for twenty minutes by ignoring the other children and playing by himself. He then started to cry, and his mother came and got him. Later the minister remarked to some of his officers, "I was trying to interest that family in our church!"

The church is usually the first place outside the home to which the small child goes. The easier this transition, the happier it is likely to be. When a church redecorated its children's rooms, using wallpaper, it had its reward when a little girl exclaimed, "It's just like home!" Unfortunately many children's rooms are anything but homelike.

The church which wins the child is almost certain to win the parents also. I have some friends who never were churchgoers and who were almost afraid of their young son, who had the characteristics of a dominant personality. When he was past two they took him to the State Street Church in Portland, Maine, with some trepidation. They feared that he would wreck the nursery, but they left him and stole away to church. It was communion Sunday and the service seemed interminable. As soon as possible, they hastened to rescue their son from the ruins of the nursery. To their surprise they found that all was well, that he liked the place, and that he did not want to go home. The only way they got him out was to promise to bring him back next Sunday—and they have been going to church ever since. That good children's rooms are a great help in building a congregation has been repeatedly demonstrated. The best approach to young parents is through their children.

The pre-school children have the greatest need for close grading and for separate rooms on an age basis. The reason for this is simple. The younger a child, the faster it grows and the more difference time makes in its capacities and powers. A three-year-old is far more different from a two-year-old than a fifteen-year-old is from a twelve-year-old. Also the smaller children get on better in small groups. A dozen are about as many as can be handled together effectively. If a church can afford it, there should be a crib room, a toddler room, a two-year, a three-year, a four-year, and a kindergarten room. If this cannot be done, there should be as much separation as possible on an age basis. When a certain church presented plans in which the crib room was in an alcove off the nursery, someone objected, "That won't work. Some of the two-year-olds will try to clean up on their competitors!"

In a previous chapter we have presented the argument for a spread-out rather than a piled-up church. The place where the spread should start is with the rooms for little children. Safety requires that their quarters be right on the ground with no steps to be stumbled up or down. Their parents fear that they will catch something; their contacts with other children should be held to a minimum. A separate entrance from the outside for each room is most desirable. There is little need for direct connection with the main building, as the parents will bring their children to the door when they arrive and claim them there when it is time to depart.

Children's rooms should not open from the sidewalk but should turn their back on the street and face a court or garden, so that in warm weather the children can play outside without danger. The church can well take a lesson from the newer public schools and make children's toilets easily accessible from each room. An economical arrangement is to place one between each two rooms.

Good accommodations for small children get abundant use. On Sunday they will be occupied at both the church school and the church hours, or during two or more church services. A New Jersey church announces that it has three services and that care and training for small children is available at all three hours. On weekdays attractive children's rooms are usually occupied by kindergartens or nursery schools. These are run on three bases. The most common is for someone to rent the accommodations. Sometimes the schools are run cooperatively by the mothers. Occasionally a church takes the responsibility of management. This is a much appreciated community service. It helps with the janitor service, but it also brings to the church building the parents who are most concerned with the welfare of their children. The first man I met, while visiting a

Philadelphia church, was the chairman of the board of trustees, of whom the minister said, "We got him through the nursery school."

Although they are our greatest opportunity, the pre-school children are not the only candidates for Christian training. Today the lower grades of the public schools are overflowing. Any church which does well by its pre-school children will soon have an abundance of first- and second-graders on its hands. These children are accustomed to larger rooms and larger groups than are their pre-school brothers and sisters. There is a little less physical activity and a little more instruction and hand work, yet this age sees rather more than it hears. It has no objection to impersonal noise. It has less need of individual classrooms than any other group.

Departmental rather than individual classrooms are now recommended by leaders in Christian education for the primary, junior, and junior high grades. These can be on either a three-year or a two-year basis. In the past the practice was to group the first, second and third grades together as the Primary Department, and the fourth, fifth, and sixth grades as the Junior Department; but one obvious objection to this arrangement was that it put first-graders, who could not read, in with third-graders who were able to read. Two-year departments are therefore becoming increasingly common, with the first two grades constituting the Primary, the third and fourth the Lower Junior, and the fifth and sixth the Upper Junior.

Under either arrangement the children of a department have their entire church school session in one large room. They assemble about an informal worship center, they use as much space as may be needed for activities and projects, and they break up into small groups for their lesson period. Under this set-up, the same floor space can be used in three different ways in the course of the morning. Not only is this sound economy, but it eliminates as well the disturbance caused by classes moving from one place to another. Departmental rooms should be at least 20' x 30', which permits their use for other purposes as well as for church school.

If such rooms cannot be obtained, a practical arrangement is to assign the Junior Department, or possibly even the Primary, to the large utility room found in most churches and usually used for dinners and other social events. A movable worship center can be placed along one wall, with the children scattering to the corners of the room for their class sessions. The classes can be separated by movable screens which have sound-absorbing surfaces; these screens can also serve for the display of teaching materials.

As the children advance through the grades, the worship becomes more formal and the content of the lesson material more important. If it is available, the upper grades can use a chapel for assembly and will profit from separate classrooms. However, they can worship in a hall and their classes can meet in the nooks and corners of the church for the lesson period. They can even use the church itself. If there are to be classrooms, they should be large enough for at least eighteen pupils. In general, the more exposed the place where a class studies, the smaller its number should be.

From the junior high grades on up the emphasis is

upon discussion, and this requires a quiet situation, which means that separate rooms are most desirable. It will be a few years before the present flood reaches these ages. One of their characteristics is a high state of gregariousness. A church either has a crowd of high school young people, or none at all. They need large rooms, but it does not follow that these should be classrooms. Church parlors and the minister's study can serve them well. Their legs and lungs are good and they are not averse to climbing. They are the people who should have the tower rooms, or that made-over coal room in the basement. If any classes must meet at the Y or some other outside place, these are the ones who can best get around.

In the South and Midwest the large adult classes are often a problem. They need separate rooms, and these are expensive. Fitting the size of the class to the size of the room is also difficult. Even though it has shrunk to a phantom of its former size, the older ladies' class may insist on keeping the room which they were assigned when they were young mothers.

If the church itself must be used for classes, it is usually better to have a number of classes—say of the junior age—occupy it, than to have an adult class monopolize the space.

The cheapest way to expand the facilities of a church is to use them twice, as we have already suggested in connection with the worship service. Most new churches must be planned with this in mind. There simply is not the money to meet the needs of today on the one-use basis which has prevailed in the past.

Double sessions of the church school can be handled in two ways.

The simplest plan is to have two complete schools, at least through junior high, with classes for all ages at both sessions. Here the early hour is likely to be more popular than the late hour, particularly with the boys who tend to put on their old clothes and disappear if Sunday school is too long postponed. One of the virtues of this plan is its utter simplicity. It requires no explaining, and all the children of a family can come at the same time. It also gives a maximum use of the facilities with a minimum of scene shifting. The only problem is recruiting the later session, which should be kept as early in the day as possible. One church tried having church and church school at ten and eleven-thirty, respectively, but soon went back to nine-thirty and eleven.

The more common but also the more difficult arrangement is to split the school on an age basis. If there is only one Sunday morning service, what usually happens is that first the pre-school classes and then the first three grades are shifted to the church hour, the older classes continuing at the usual hour. The reason for this is that the smaller children are all brought, and so can come when their parents go to church, while those from the fourth grade up can get around on their feet or on bikes in many communities.

If a church has two services and the school is divided on an age basis, the younger children should come at the early hour. They are by nature early risers and are experts at getting their parents up also. The older children go to picture shows and otherwise indulge themselves on Saturday night, and so are sleepier on Sunday morning and more favorably disposed towards the later hour.

Where a church has only one church service but two church school sessions the question always arises, How can the teachers who work during the second session attend church? The assumption that all teachers always attend church has scant basis in fact, although in small churches the teachers often double in the choir. The best answer is that given by a pastor: "I am certain that the teachers derive more spiritual benefit from presenting Christian truth to their pupils than they would get from listening to me." In one instance the minister seeks to compensate the teachers who miss his Sunday morning service by conducting a special study class for them during the week—which they appreciate. Another procedure is to recruit teachers on the basis of teaching half a year and going to church for the other half.

Another objection to the church school which is divided on an age basis is the family which has children in both sessions. If it goes to church, such a family is no worse off with two church school sessions than it was with church school and church at different hours. With compact parishes the older children can usually get to the early session without too much trouble. The real difficulty is with the families which come from a distance. The ultimate answer is to have two sessions of the church as well as of the church school.

Dividing a school on an age basis presents some problems in the use of equipment. The most differentiated rooms are those designed for the pre-school children. If at all possible, these should be used at both hours by pre-school children, of whom there are usually an abundance. If this cannot be done, older groups might use these quarters with the minimum of disturbance of the furniture—and no loss of dignity by the young people. But don't try to put a first- or second-grader in a kindergarten room. The tables and chairs which serve for the primary grades can be used by the juniors without too great inconvenience. As for other equipment, adequate storage is the prime problem.

Visual aids are being used increasingly in the church school. These depend for their effectiveness upon the availability of a really dark room. This requires the minimum of windows and the maximum of shades. The best answer is to equip one room for the daylight showing of pictures and then to rotate its use.

In earlier pages we have stated the case for the spread-out, one-floor church. From the point of view of the church school, it has two virtues. It will provide more and better sound separation than can be had in a two-level building. It can be added to with the minimum of trouble and expense. This is most important for the church school.

The present age graph with the heavy enrollment in the pre-school classes obviously will not last. We suspect that what will happen is that there will be no diminution in the numbers of young children, but a great increase in those of older ages. Much depends upon how successful the church school is in winning the interest of the children and in stirring the imagination of their parents. We know what we need now, but there is no way of telling what the pressures will be ten years from now. The sensible procedure is to get plenty of land, to make what we build now as flexible as possible, and to leave an abundance of room for those who follow us to erect what they need.

Most congregations need to have the problems of the church school visualized for them. Figures and abstract statements mean little. They need to see something. Here is a plan which has proved most helpful.

The present enrollment with some allowance for growth was broken down into age groups and departments and then multiplied by the floor space recommended, which ranged from 35 square feet for a three-year-old to 20 for a junior child. Sheets of paper were then cut to size, using the scale of half an inch for a foot. There were six of these: the smallest for a crib room, a modest toddler room, a larger three-year-old room, a sizable kindergarten room which could be divided if necessary, a big primary room, and a somewhat smaller junior room.

The land available was then measured and laid out on the same scale on a carpeted floor, using string held down by Scotch tape for the boundaries. The next step was to arrange, and then re-arrange, the rooms on what was fortunately a spacious lot. At once the group began to see possibilities for a sheltered walk and some landscaping—and for economies in the use of outside doors in place of indoor corridors. A number of combinations were tried.

Some of the reactions were surprising. Quarters for the junior department had been added tentatively, as it could be accommodated elsewhere, but the prevailing opinion was that it should be retained. The group felt that a double garage on the property was in the way and should be removed. Most significant of all was the comment, "If we do this, we will attract a lot more children; where shall we put them?" It was pointed out that the best answer was not larger rooms but more of them, and that there would still be room for considerable expansion. There was the added suggestion that the original assignment of rooms would probably be changed anyhow in the course of time, that what was needed was the utmost flexibility, and this could better be achieved with a group of one-story rooms than in a multi-level building. What actually happened was that the group sold itself on a larger plan than the one which had been suggested to them.

Chapter 12

A "HOMEY FEELING" FOR YOUR CHURCH

Two reasons bring people to church: a yearning to know God and an active desire to meet their friends. The Protestant church has been an exceedingly folksy institution. The people came early to see one another, they lingered afterwards to exchange greetings and gossip, and all too often this chattiness impinged upon the service itself. Preachers cultivated an informal approach, taking delight in giving out the notices. Straight pews made way for circular ones so that everybody could see who was there without straining the muscles of the neck.

Recent years have evidenced an increasing emphasis on worship. For an awe-inspiring service quiet is essential, with the attention of the people centered on something more than themselves. This can only be achieved by separating worship from the highly social atmosphere in which it has commonly been involved. Here the peril is that in concentrating our thought on God we may forget our fellow men. The solution to this problem is not to discourage sociability in connection with the services of the church but to arrange a time and supply a place where Protestants can exercise their garrulous instincts. The more we emphasize worship, the more necessary does it become that we provide social facilities also.

Two other factors enter the situation.

The American home is getting smaller. The trend is to omit the dining room and eat in either a nook off the kitchen or in a corner of the living room. We no longer have room for much company. Groups which once met in homes are now compelled to gather at the church. The home wedding is almost a thing of the past.

The weekday use of our churches is constantly growing. With the passing of the midweek meeting and the decline in lectures and entertainments, there are probably fewer formal gatherings, but over against this has been a proliferation of committee and group meetings of various sorts. The doors of our churches swing open more than ever. If there is an attractive room furnished in a way that invites informal meetings in a convenient location, it will become the destination of most of the weekday traffic.

The impulse to worship and the instinct for friendliness are close kin, and it is entirely normal for each to stimulate the other. Historically the starting point for the social life of a church has been in connection with its worship, which is as it should be. In the past, and in milder climates today, this centers in the church yard. The Scotch economize on words while in the kirk, but will let dinner get cold while they talk to one another on the sidewalk. In the rural South "dinner on the grounds" is a happy aftermath to "preaching Sunday."

This after-church sociability is gradually being gotten under cover, with a strong assist from the weather in northern latitudes. This began by increasing the space for what the architects call "circulation" either at the back of the church or in the entryway. The next step was to furnish this area in a homey, informal fashion.

Then came the parlor-narthex. Obviously people needed quite a bit of room in which to get in and out of church on Sunday. This should be a friendly place. By enlarging it a bit and furnishing it like a parlor it could be used during the week in the latter capacity. For small and medium-size churches this has proven most popular. They got a parlor for little more than the cost of an adequate entrance, and they soon found that the central location of this social room was most convenient.

Some of the larger churches are giving this idea a further development. The First Congregational Church in DeKalb, Illinois, has a large general entrance from which the worshipers pass through a parlor complete with fireplace, kitchenette, and picture window on their way into the place of worship. The First Baptist Church in Flint, Michigan, has a large rotunda-narthex from which open both the church and the church parlor.

The importance of making the parlor central to both the physical layout and the life of a church can hardly be overstressed. Too often we have had "ladies' parlors" tucked away in the far recesses of a building and frequently kept locked, to prevent the young people from wearing out the upholstery. Such rooms may serve as a place of pilgrimage for high teas and similar esoteric events, but they cannot function the way the social rooms of a church should if they are to serve their true ends of promoting friendliness.

Our conception of the parlor in a church is close to that of the lobby in a good small hotel. This should be the place where people come and go. Here they should gather for almost any purpose, and then go directly to the church for worship, to the church offices to see the minister or on other business, or to the parish hall for dinners or other gatherings. That is, the parlor should be the central place of welcome for all the activities of the church. We grant that this is not always easy to arrange, particularly if the conventional lines of church architecture are followed, but we believe that it is an ideal worth working toward. Over against the barren institutionalism which so often prevails, the first impression made on anyone who enters a church for any reason should be friendly. If the entryway is not parlorized, the parlor itself should be close at hand and open at all times.

What are the functions that such a room should serve?

First of all, it should be a place of welcome to all comers, whether church-bound or on other errands. It should say, "We're glad to see you; take your ease" to those who are attending the church for the first time, to the couple coming to arrange for their wedding, to the distraught soul seeking counsel from the minister, and even to those on business errands.

It should be a meeting place for boards and committees. The atmosphere in which church officers gather has much to do with the attitude in which they approach the business in hand. A barren place invites a barren meeting, while it is hard to be stubborn in a relaxed atmosphere.

Group meetings of the women and of the young people should be held here. We enhance the self-respect of boys and girls when we invite them to use an attractive room.

A conveniently located social hall invites receptions, teas, and coffee hours after the services of the church and in connection with weddings.

If it is not a general runway this room should also be used by one of the older and larger church school classes. Happy surroundings encourage the learning process far more than do blackboards and a school-room atmosphere.

A room which is used in such varied ways must be versatile in its furnishing. Everything should be easily movable with ample storage space immediately available. The basic furniture should be sturdy because it will receive hard usage. This is no place for anything dainty or fragile. Tea tables should be reserved for tea time. In addition to the easy, comfortable chairs there should be a good supply of folding metal chairs in a nearby closet. Facilities should be available for serving light refreshments—unless the church kitchen is nearby. Little more than a hot plate, a tap, and storage space for glasses, cups, etc., is really needed. Unless a kitchenette is kept within small compass, the church will find itself with a second kitchen on its hands, which is wasteful. A fireplace, windows, floor lamps, gay drapes are all desirable. How religious the pictures and other decorations should be is an open question. The purpose of the room is quite human and we rather doubt if the worship element should be introduced.

As we have suggested, one of the functions which has been quite generally transferred from the home to the church is the wedding. While there is no perceptible increase in elaborate church weddings such as flourish in the movies, the young people of today would generally prefer to be married in church if this can be done conveniently and without too great an expense. Protestantism owes it to its young people to provide facilities which will meet this need without taxing their pocketbooks.

For a church wedding three things are needful.

The bride should be able to dress at the church. Wedding parties often come from a distance. For a bride to array herself in a hotel room or even her own home and then be driven to the church exposes her to the scrutiny of bystanders in an embarrassing manner. Almost inevitably some final touches will be added at the church. The better arrangement is for her, together with her feminine attendants, to dress there. At the least this calls for a glorified powder room, at the most a distinctive bride's room. The churches which have such facilities find them exceedingly popular.

The second requirement is a place for the wedding itself. This can be in a chapel or even a parlor, but the better arrangement is to take one's wedding vows in the same place that the congregation assembles for worship from Sunday to Sunday. Here the prime requirement is a center aisle of sufficient width for a portly father and a well-nourished bride to walk down without brushing against the pews. At the head of the aisle should be steps leading up to the communion table. The best arrangement is for the couple to take the preliminary or betrothal vows on the floor of the church and then for the contracting parties and their two attendants to proceed up the steps to the table for the final vows.

Elaborate decorations for weddings should be discouraged. We suspect that in the past their real function was to conceal the essential ugliness of many church interiors. A really good church does not need to be dolled up for the marriage ceremony. It is a good idea for the governing board to adopt a rule limiting what can be done. One good bouquet is often enough.

The third requirement for a wedding is a place for the reception, and this should be in the church. There is no way in which many people can be invited to the church and a favored few to a reception at some other place without offending someone. The better way is to have both the wedding and the reception at the church. This also takes care of the problem of alcoholic refreshments. What is needed is a parlor of appropriate size conveniently located so that the guests can easily make their way to it. In many churches the women's organization does the catering for weddings. They make a little money but also have a wonderful time. This is a service which the bride's family greatly appreciates. Getting weddings out of the homes and into the churches is prolonging the lives of the mothers of the brides, and protecting the solvency of their fathers. And it is associating one of life's most solemn moments with the church.

Chapter **13**

A PROPER HABITATION FOR THE MINISTER

IN ABOUT half the churches visited, the following speech is pertinent.

"Your next minister will refuse to live in your parsonage. He will be young, and he will have a wife who is both young and attractive. She will survey the old house in which your old ministers have lived and say, 'Do you expect me to keep all of these big rooms clean? I wouldn't have time for anything else. And bring up my children right in the heart of town with a fire house and a bus station for neighbors? We can't do that!' and so you will hurry off and get a new parsonage. Why don't you do it now?"

We have almost as many antiquated homes for the minister as we have obsolete churches. Large numbers of both will be replaced in the next few years.

Where should the parsonage be located?

Alongside the church, or even connected with it, is the traditional and ready answer. This makes it easy for anyone to find the minister. It permits him to keep an eye on the property and make good the deficiencies of the janitor. This is handy for the congregation.

It is also the arrangement preferred by the Roman Catholic Church. In contrast to Protestant practice, there are no offices in the church building. The business of the parish is conducted in the rectory, and this is next to the church, for the convenience of everybody, including the younger clergy who are assigned to the early masses and must get to church early in the day.

Protestant ministers have wives and children, who often object to living in a goldfish bowl subject to inspection by their church members at any time. Most ministers prefer to live away from the church, and the younger they are, the stronger their convictions on this matter. The pastor of a church can rarely escape from the responsibilities of his position, but at least he can remove himself from its physical shadow for his hours of relaxation. To go away from home for their work builds the morale of most men.

Many church people are obsessed with the idea that the only proper place to build a parsonage is next door to the church. Before this is done two questions should be faced. Will the church need this space for future expansion? Too often the minister lives right where the educational building should be. Would the bank make a commercial loan for a residence on this site? In other words, is the proposed parsonage a sound investment? If the church is in the center of town or is surrounded by old property which has seen its best days, the answer will be No! Or putting it another way, the parsonage should have a location where almost any member of the congregation would be glad to live.

The size and character of the parsonage will depend upon the type of community which the church serves.

The larger the city, the less will there be to distinguish the parsonage from the other homes of the parish. In the metropolitan centers the minister is not expected to put up visiting speakers for the night. Unless he is so inclined, there is little pressure on him to entertain. He and his family live much as do their church members.

The smaller the community, the greater the pressure on the parsonage. Where there are no hotels and few eating places, the mistress of the manse must take in all and sundry. Most town and country churches have few social facilities. Many meetings which in the city would be held in the church must from necessity take place in the parsonage.

We once read in a Canadian church paper, "The first requirement of a manse is that it keep the minister warm." This is particularly true of our northern neighbors, who commonly leave their storm windows on the year around. To paraphrase this statement for use south of the border, "The first requirement of a parsonage is that it keep the minister and his family comfortable." It should be first of all a good place to live.

The minister's wife has a dual role. She is both the wife of a man and a community personality. More is expected of her than of most women, both in the home and out of it. And the smaller the community, and the larger the parsonage, the greater are the demands made upon her. A well seasoned pastor's wife can produce a tasty meal out of most anything on minimum notice, but it takes years to master this art. The young ones have both more babies and more troubles. Both the young and the old are entitled to the maximum of labor-saving arrangements and devices. A modern kitchen for the parsonage is a good investment for any church. The quicker the woman of the house can get through her cleaning and cooking, the more time will she have to assist her husband.

In planning a parsonage there are a number of specific needs, which we will list in the order of their universality and urgency.

Ample clothes closets handy to the door are a prime requisite. A minister should be able to receive from one to a dozen people without either piling up their wraps or sending them upstairs, which may not be ready to receive them.

The dining area should be located so as not to be visible from the reception hall. People come at all sorts of hours, some of them strange. If the family is enjoying a meal, it is awkward to either invite them to join it or to leave them out. The answer is for the family to eat where it cannot be seen.

A short cut from the kitchen to the front door is most desirable, but with a good door in between. The woman of the house should be able to get to the door with the fewest possible steps.

A downstairs toilet is obviously desirable. It will save steps for the family and make it unnecessary for visitors to intrude on the more private portions of the house.

How much of a study should be provided in the

parsonage depends upon the nature of the community, and also the habits and disposition of the minister. There are two reasons why it is better for a minister to do his work and meet people in the church rather than at his home: less involvement in household duties and greater accessibility to those who seek him. To this there are two possible exceptions.

Wherever they live, some men will want a hide-out where they can do intensive study and work on their sermons. Their aim is to get away from people. For this purpose an upstairs room in the parsonage is as good as any.

A wise person has observed, "City people tell you all about themselves but nothing about their neighbors; country people tell you all about their neighbors but nothing about themselves." Because of the surveillance on the part of their neighbors and friends to which they are subject, those who live in small places are reluctant to tell their troubles to anyone. Rural ministers do little counseling. Those who do seek them out would probably prefer to be making a social call at the parsonage than to be seen seeking a private interview in the church. In small communities a good place for the study is on the ground floor of the parsonage, with a separate entrance if possible.

A parsonage should be well supplied with bedrooms. Ministers have always had rather more children than their members, and recent studies indicate that their families are getting larger. Three bedrooms should be the minimum anywhere. Those who have few children, or whose children have grown, can usually put the extra rooms to good use. In the cities, where visiting officials prefer to stop at hotels, a guest room is optional; in the smaller places it is almost a necessity.

The parsonage should be a source of pride to the parish. While not a mansion, it should be a bit larger and better than the average of the homes of the congregation, simply because the minister is expected to meet the well-to-do on a basis of social equality and because his home must often supplement the facilities which the church may lack.

Parsonages are relatively easy to secure. Sometimes families which have either petered out or departed to the city bequeath the old homestead to the church for a parsonage. In such cases they should be asked for an endowment to provide for the upkeep; otherwise ministers who must live amidst the departed glory of another day are decidedly out of luck. On the other hand, churches seem to experience surprisingly little difficulty in financing new parsonages. Everybody can see the necessity of a place for the minister to live.

Chapter 14

WHERE MANY GROUPS WILL GATHER

EVERY congregation needs a utility room suitable for dinners, the church school, general gatherings, and recreation.

Traditionally this has been the church basement. This means that the size and shape of the church upstairs has set the pattern for the size and shape of the room downstairs, which may not have been what was needed at all. The ceiling height has been another difficulty. If this was kept low, the room itself is necessarily dark and gloomy. If the ceiling is given a proper height either the church must be elevated above the ground or the parish hall sunk in the ground. In either case much climbing will be required of somebody, either up into the church or down into the basement. Neither is desirable.

The parish hall cannot come into its own until it gets out of the ground and on the same level with the other rooms of the church. Then it can be the size and shape which its use requires and it can be related to other rooms in ways that are helpful; the church parlor serving as a reception room for church dinners, multi-use of the kitchen for the serving of refreshments, the sharing of toilets.

The first question to be settled about such a room is its size, and here the controlling factor is its use as a dining hall. What is the maximum number of people, you must decide, who will dine together at one time? This is a real puzzle. Fundamentally it is a matter of policy to be decided by the church.

The women will present several arguments for a large dining room. The first of these is often, "That is where we make our money." The answer is that the profit on church dinners is largely imaginary, and that when people come just to eat they can be fed in relays. A better case can be made for an occasional large banquet—the mother-daughter dinner, the high school alumni banquet, the occasional denominational meeting which must be entertained. Here two questions should be raised. The first is, How often do these events occur? It is ridiculous to let something which happens once a year, or sometimes less often, control the arrangement of space which the church school uses every week. Yet we have known of churches which were "built to entertain the conference." The second question is the availability of other dining facilities in the community. If the high school cafeteria or the town hall can be used for the occasional big dinner, there is no sense in duplicating these facilities. If one church in a town has a big dining room it is usually willing to rent or loan it to other churches for their special occasions. Once a fire broke out in a

Congregational church while the women were brewing a mother-daughter banquet, and they picked up their things and moved into the Methodist church where they had just as good a time as would have been enjoyed in their own church. This should happen more frequently and without benefit of fires. Churches should not duplicate facilities which are used only semi-occasionally. Here is a chance for some practical ecumenicity.

The argument against the large dining room is primarily financial. The law commonly requires ten square feet for each person seated at a table for a meal. The rock bottom minimum for which a parish hall can be built is $10 a square foot, with $12.50 as more nearly average. Up to a point the space used for dining will also be utilized for the church school and other activities, but it should be borne in mind that anything beyond these needs will cost $125 for each diner accommodated—and it will take a good many years to accumulate that much profit on the occasional big dinner.

The current trend is away from the big banquet but toward the multiplication of small lunches and dinners. The current generation of women is less disposed to exhaust themselves working over hot stoves than were their mothers, while eating out is less of a novelty for their menfolks than formerly. And yet we have seen the statement that the churches are now serving more meals than are the hotels. (If this be true, it is due in part to the decline of the small town hotel.) What is increasing is the meal with a purpose. We were once the guest at a dinner put on by six couples in a country church. The food was delicious and was entirely consumed, while the company was hilarious; yet some real business was taken care of most effectively. The committee or board that eats together is likely to do a better job of thinking together. These small, intimate affairs build the fellowship of the church more than do the larger and more formal occasions. A couple of dozen people will get better acquainted than will 200.

Once the capacity of the hall has been decided, it should then be planned so as to take care of that number of people effectively. The size of the tables and the way they are to be arranged should be worked out before the dimensions of the room are set. Here are two rules which may be helpful. The space allowed from center of table to center of table, or center of aisle to center of aisle is seven feet, while two feet should be allowed for each person seated. This works out at seven square feet per person, which is below the legal requirement of ten square feet, but the difference will be absorbed in aisles and other free space. Round tables promote more sociability than do square ones, but they also take up more room. Both the number and size of the tables and where they are to be stored when not in use, should be decided before the architect goes to work on his final plans.

Not as much preliminary planning is possible for the church school use of a parish hall as for dining. A limit can be set to the number of people who will eat together, but no one can tell how many children the future will bring, or what their age groupings may be. The aim should be the maximum flexibility in the use of the available space. The most important factor is storage. Space should be worked out before the room is built for the screens, tables, and small chairs which the church school may need for its work. The disadvantage of using a parish hall with Primary children is that they require smaller chairs and lower tables than will be used in the room at other times. On the other hand, Juniors can use standard size tables and chairs, but they also gain more from meeting in separate rooms, if these are available.

For both dining and class work an acoustical ceiling is most desirable. It will greatly reduce the strain on the teachers. On the other hand, acoustical treatment will deaden the music and compel a speaker either to shout or use some sort of amplification. A reasonable amount of sound-absorbent material will probably add more to the usefulness of the room than it will subtract from it.

The third use for a parish hall is public meetings which cannot properly be held in the church, and entertainments of all sorts. Thanks to radio and television, both are declining. Speeches and shows are becoming increasingly air-borne. Many churches imagine that at some time in the future they will go in for amateur dramatics, but this day rarely comes. If these efforts are of a religious character and the church has an ample chancel, that is where they belong. For the others, the cheapest and most satisfactory arrangement is to hire a hall. In planning a parish hall as a place of assembly two problems must be faced. The first is to decide how many chairs will be needed and where they are to be kept, and the second is whether or not to build a stage. The usual experience is that the stage is the least used feature of the churches that have them. Usually they serve two functions: as a classroom without benefit of light or sound separation, and as a convenient place for the storage of tables. Both of these needs can be taken care of more economically in other ways. If the demand for a stage cannot be denied, remember that it will be used for worship as much as anything, and keep the height low. Most existing church stages are altogether too high, probably to take care of those tables! However, a low platform, preferably movable, will meet most of the needs of a parish hall. This is in accord with the present emphasis on the "theater in the round," in which the audience and the actors are brought closer together without benefit of footlights.

The fourth use for the parish hall will be recreation. Here some clear thinking is needed.

Despite unfavorable experience in the past, there is a persistent demand for church gymnasiums, often with the argument, "We should do something to keep the young people off the streets," where they are rarely found these days! Put a bit more subtly the reasoning will be, "If we are going to have a hall, why not extend the walls up a bit further and get a combination hall-gymnasium such as many high schools have, particularly in the smaller places?" Actually, the only sport requiring a high ceiling is basketball, which is a game that only ten boys can play at a time, but which takes up a lot of room. Basketball is hard on the walls and ceilings—which must be hard surfaces if they are to survive—as well as on the light fixtures of a room. Hard surfaces plus a high ceiling produce a difficult place in which to speak and a noisy place in which to eat. Rare is the gym which has any eye appeal. The sensible policy is to let the schools and the Y's take care of basketball. For a church this sport costs far more than it is worth.

A parish hall with a reasonable ceiling height and adequate storage facilities can take care of the other recreational needs of a congregation. All most indoor games require is an abundance of floor space. This is particularly true of square dancing, which is now widely prevalent. Instead of erecting a recreational building, churches should so plan that their parish hall has storage for all the paraphernalia which needs to be gotten out of the way—the chairs used for dinners, meetings, and church schools; the tables used for dinners and the church school; possibly even the platform. The economical and easy way to multiply the usefulness of a parish hall is to carefully plan a place where everything can be put away. This should not be left to the architect, or to be worked out later. Somebody needs to be exceedingly vigilant at this point. It may sound strange, but the place to begin with the planning of a parish hall is with the storage, because nothing can contribute more to its success.

How about the scouts of both sexes? Most churches have them—and the highly proper people in the congregation blame them for all the dirt that gets into a church and for most of the wear and tear on the furniture. On behalf of the boys in particular we would like to offer a counter-charge—that the churches do not commonly provide them with proper facilities.

What the scouts really need is plenty of open floor

space and somewhere to put their equipment. If a church has a basement, this is where the scout room belongs. In mild climates this can even be a cabin out behind. Unless a church has a lot of money, or a scoutmaster who likes to build a monument to himself, the sensible arrangement is to provide a meeting and storage room, if possible; if not, a storage room, and in either case to let the scouts (both kinds) use the parish hall for their games during cold weather. This, again, is primarily a matter of storage.

How about the outside organizations which will want to use the parish hall for their meetings? If the church is in a new community, there will be some requests of this nature from various organizations, but these decline as the years pass. The amount of good which this does a church is greatly exaggerated. The real justification is the service which it renders the community.

The plain truth is that few if any outside or community organizations contribute enough to a church to pay for their keep in terms of light, heat, and janitor service. A church is a religious institution and should never picture itself as anything else. Community service should be a by-product of its other activities. It should meet such needs as it conveniently can, but this should not be its primary aim.

Chapter 15

ENCOURAGING THE CULINARY ARTS

ALTHOUGH the kitchen is an adjunct to the parish hall, it seems wise to discuss it separately.

The virtue of a kitchen does not consist in its size but in its organization. In the past, church kitchens just happened. The sink and the stove were put by the drain and the chimney respectively, and other features fitted in wherever there was space. Many church kitchens are too large for efficiency, perhaps with the idea of keeping the girls slim by giving them plenty of running around to do. Often there are bottlenecks. One church explained that a large woman in a certain spot could immobilize the whole place. Nowhere is careful planning and even research more needed than in laying out a church kitchen. This should begin with the types of meals to be served.

At present the covered dish or potluck supper appears to be the most popular of church repasts, particularly in the smaller churches. This calls for a table or counter on which the food is placed, a warming oven, and dishwashing facilities. In many cases the people bring their own dishes and utensils with them. The major objection to this type of meal is the waste of food involved. Even though the men, at least, eat more than they should, there is much left over. Also, the cost is unevenly distributed. We predict that this type will become less common.

The small dinner prepared at the church either as a whole or in part is increasing. We suspect that the easier it is to prepare such meals the more of them there will be. The ideal church kitchen should inspire every woman who sees it with a desire to get up a meal. This also holds for the preparation of refreshments. We believe that the normal use of the church kitchen in the future will be to serve anywhere from a dozen to a hundred people either a "bite" or a full meal.

We have discussed the decline of the dinner for profit and the big occasion in connection with the size of the dining room. These big affairs will undoubtedly continue and should be provided for in ways that we will point out, but this should not be regarded as the primary purpose of either the parish hall or the kitchen.

If many people are to be served, much of the food must be prepared some time in advance, which calls for both warming ovens and refrigerating facilities. The longer use of a medium-size kitchen can be made to do for a larger one. During the actual serving of the meal only the hot food should be handled in the kitchen. Juices and drinks, salads and desserts can be taken care of elsewhere. A big meal gains by decentralization of activity.

Our further discussion will have in mind a kitchen

which can easily serve 100 people but which can take care of twice as many in a pinch. In the actual operation of a church kitchen there are four problems.

The first is the separation of the waitresses from the food-handlers in the kitchen, who may or may not be the people who did the cooking. Here the serving counter is essential. As this is the most frequent bottleneck, it should be of ample size. It may open directly into the parish hall, or onto a corridor leading to the hall. The latter is more expensive, but also the more desirable. It can be so arranged that meals can be served in other rooms besides the large dining room, which is often desirable. After a meal it keeps the clatter of the dishes from intruding upon any program which may follow.

A second problem is the routing of the food from the place of storage by way of the places of preparation to the serving counter. Here some thought should be given to how much of the work is to be done at the church. If the women start with the raw materials, the place to begin is with a refrigerator and a sink where vegetables can be washed. From these facilities a working counter should extend to the stove, and another counter from the stove to the serving counter. In a church kitchen, working space is far more important than open floor space. There should be the minimum of carrying and the maximum of passing along. An oblong room is likely to be more efficient than a square one.

The dirty dishes are the third matter to be considered. They should be kept as separate as possible from the clean ones. In restaurants and some churches there is a separate counter or even room for the dirty dishes. The necessity for this depends upon how meals are served. In a church where all eat at once the only problem is to keep the desserts and the dirty dishes apart. Often the serving counter can also function as the receiving place for returning "empties." In either case the facilities for washing the dishes should be near at hand so as to reduce the handling to a minimum.

Ultimately, churches will be held to the same sanitary requirements which commercial eating establishments must meet. Ohio and Wisconsin are two states we know are working toward this end. In Frederick County, Maryland, and in the town of Trumbull, Connecticut, health officers inspect the churches regularly. Actually, in any community the local authorities can classify churches as "public eating places," and apply the law accordingly. Any church which is building a new kitchen or remodeling an old one would be wise to meet the local requirements for sanitation. Usually this means either a three-divisional deep sink with one section for washing, another for rinsing, and a third for scalding, or a mechanical dishwasher.

The location of these facilities should be carefully studied. A common mistake is to put them out in the middle of the floor, which means that the dirty dishes must be carried to them and the clean ones carried away. What is needed is plenty of room on one side for the dirty dishes and on the other for the clean ones. The larger the counter space on either side the better.

The fourth problem of a church kitchen is storage. In the past the idea often was to keep the dishes well-locked so nobody could steal them, and the result was closets in which it was difficult for more than one woman to get at a time. The present thought is to store the dishes and utensils as close as possible to the spot where they will be needed. As the food progresses from the stove to the serving counter, it should meet the receptacles in which it is to be placed. Planning all this calls for the abundant use of brain power. All sorts of ideas will emerge: drawers for the knives, forks, and spoons which can be opened from either the kitchen or the outside, locating the coffee urn and the cups and saucers near each other, the use of carts for the distribution of glasses and plates. Ingenuity can save much labor and produce smooth functioning at dinner time.

Labeling the places where the various things are to be kept is most helpful. The writer does much talking in churches and is by nature a thirsty animal. Locating the glasses in an ordinary kitchen involves opening many cupboard doors. He found one church where an imaginative soul had pasted pictures of what was kept within on each door so that illiterates, people with weak eyes, and folks in a hurry could get what they wanted.

In general the storage cabinets in a church kitchen should be above and below the working counters. This gets the dishes near where they will be needed and also keeps down congestion both in putting things away and getting them again. This means that wall space is at a premium in a kitchen, which is another argument for a long and relatively narrow room.

Most churches which have steam tables make relatively little use of them, because church meals are commonly served simultaneously. If a good timetable has been worked out for the cooking, it should be served immediately.

Natural light is desirable in a kitchen, with the space above the sinks the best place for windows. There should also be strong artificial light.

Sound control in a church kitchen is an almost insoluble problem. The work itself is noisy, and the people who do it are garrulous, but the law commonly prohibits acoustical ceilings because they absorb grease as well as sound and constitute a fire hazard.

The floor covering should be grease-resistant and somewhat resilient, as cooking is not a sedentary occupation.

An outside door for the reception of groceries, with a drive handy is most desirable.

Here are two luxury items for a church kitchen: a red ceiling which will make the women look rosy, and a dressing room where they can change from cooking togs to other apparel.

Chapter **16**

WHERE MUCH WORK GETS DONE

UNTIL recent years most churches were empty tombs between religious services—and some still are. We know of a churchgoing dog who napped too long on Sunday morning and did not get out until Monday afternoon. Formerly his incarceration would have lasted until prayer meeting night!

Today most new churches include an office in the first unit. Even though money is scarce and their space is overtaxed, they consider it essential that there be a weekday center for the direction of church activity. It is also true that in terms of hours occupied, the office, or offices, are the most used part of a church.

The reasons for this change are significant. Churches are increasing their activities and in consequence are taking themselves more seriously. This means that the minister has more to do, and needs more help if he is to get it done. This should begin with a place in which to work.

If he is about the house, only a tough-minded and

brutish minister can keep from becoming entangled in domestic matters, particularly if his wife is young and they are blessed with an abundance of children. Study is ever an urgent matter, but if the wife gets a phone call while she is bathing the baby only a hard-hearted husband can refuse to heed her cry for help. Housekeeping is a series of crises, a succession of deadlines to be met. Absence is the only acceptable alibi. If a man isn't there, the wife, the children, and dinner will still survive. A minister has a far better chance of getting his work done if he can leave home every morning like the man next door and take himself to the equivalent of a place of business, and the world accords him increased respect when he does this.

Pastoral counseling is becoming an increasingly important part of the minister's service to church and community. If he is to help people with their problems he must be accessible to them. The greater their need, the more timid they often are. For a serious discussion it is far better for them to come to the minister than for him to come to them. Only under circumstances of extreme urgency will they seek him at his home. There they feel that they are intruding, and they fear that the wife and children may be overly aware of their presence. Most people will unburden themselves more freely in a church than anywhere else. There they seem to feel something of the sanctity of the Catholic confessional.

A minister needs working space for three quite different types of activity.

A place where he can study, really think, and prepare his sermons is essential, but often difficult to achieve. Men of different temperaments will work in different ways. Some ministers will want to find peace and quiet in a hideout of some sort; this *can* be at home. Large churches can sometimes provide an unpublicized study in some remote nook in the edifice. Most men will probably have to do their sermon preparation in an office used for other purposes, but at a time which is somewhat protected.

For effective counseling the people who come to see a minister need to be put at ease. They must be protected against both eavesdropping and interruption. The minister must be unhurried and relaxed. If possible, the room should not look "busy." The minister's desk should be informal rather than executive. The chairs should be easy, the lighting moderate. It should be possible for visitors to come and go without being too conspicuous. Some churches can provide a room designed for this purpose alone but usually this is not possible. If there is a parlor which is not too conspicuous, it may be possible to take people there. In matters of extreme urgency, where utter privacy is the first requirement, a minister can make use of some remote room. At such times the furnishings do not matter.

The minister is also the head of an organization. The burdens of church administration are sometimes exaggerated, yet every minister must both plan and persuade. The smaller the church, the more is he involved in the details. It has been seriously suggested that the seminaries train their students in the operation of mimeograph machines, as that will be one of their major occupations immediately after graduation. In the larger churches he must direct the work of a paid staff. All of this is best done from a well-equipped office.

In the larger churches the number of people employed in the work of the church has expanded beyond anything the church architects of the past ever dreamed of. Even churches built during the last thirty years are oftentimes entirely lacking in adequate office facilities.

In the light of these considerations, where and what should the church offices be? Obviously they will vary greatly with the size and character of the congregation.

Ready accessibility is the first requirement for church offices. Often have we gone into old churches, listened for some sound which might indicate where the minister or secretary might be found, and then stumbled around until we discovered their hiding place. One of the weakest thoughts which have ever plagued architects has been to put the choir room on one side of the chancel and the minister's study on the other—and this is still being done. The idea seems to be that after a minister has written a sermon he should be expected to take only a minimum number of steps to the spot where he will deliver it. This is the worst possible place for both minister and choir because the space is never sufficient to really take care of them, and because of the difficulty of getting to these quarters. We also object to going up an alley or around to the back of a church to see the minister. The suggestion is that one is sneaking in.

The best place for the church office is immediately off the main weekday entrance to the building. Most churches are rather large buildings with contents of considerable value. Somebody should know who is coming and going and what they are up to. When visitors arrive, they should be received and given whatever direction they need. In a small church the minister will have to discharge this responsibility, at least when he is around. In large churches it is the job of the church secretary or receptionist. In any case there should be a doorkeeper in the House of the Lord, and the place for that functionary is near the door. The minimum requirement for any church is an office which "covers" the most used entrance.

The number of offices and the degree of their differentiation will depend upon the size and financial resources of a church. If a minister and secretary are all that can be afforded, the secretary should have the front office and the minister the one behind it. If there are several members of the staff, both economy and efficiency will be increased if they can be grouped together with ready access from one to another. Our experience is that the utility of a secretary or an assistant is in almost direct proportion of their proximity. To have to make a summons on the phone or to go on a pilgrimage to get a letter dictated or a memo drawn up is a waste of time and energy.

The refinement of church offices can be carried to almost any degree, but there is one matter which should be given relatively early attention. Most churches do a lot of what might be called amateur printing of one sort or another. This is a messy business, and also requires considerable space for storage. As soon as possible it should be removed from public view to a workroom. If possible this should be handy, but if necessary it can be upstairs and out of the way.

Chapter 17

HOW ABOUT A CHAPEL?

THE necessity for a chapel depends upon the character of your church.

If your church is of a moderate size with an effective center of worship so that an individual can come in and pray by himself without embarrassment or undue self-consciousness, your need for a chapel is not urgent. In such a room a small wedding will not be lost, and there is a considerable gain in having such events in the same place that the congregation regularly assembles for worship. This is also the proper place for baptisms, which should be a rite in which the congregation shares. If the communion table and cross are dominant and claim the attention of the worshipers, a small group will not feel out of place in your church.

On the other hand, if your church is over-size, ugly, and lacking in worshipful atmosphere, a chapel is very much in order. Many of the churches which we have inherited are suited to just one thing—a big Sunday morning preaching service. To a lesser degree, this can be said of some of our larger new churches. Where the individual finds himself lost against the bigness of the setting, some more intimate place for worship is needed.

A chapel should not be just a miniature church, a place of refuge for the congregation when heat is scarce or numbers few. A chapel should not be a lecture hall nor a place for group discussions. Its one purpose should be worship. We would suggest the following uses.

If the church is unsuitable, the chapel should serve for weddings, possibly funerals, Lenten services, and any small gathering of a religious nature. In a new church this should not be necessary.

A chapel is an excellent place for the worship of the Junior and Junior High Departments of the church school. These ages are most responsive to the mood that such a room can create. An excellent arrangement is to have one age group use the chapel for the first twenty minutes of the church school period and the other for the last twenty minutes. This will reduce the amount of space needed for departmental assemblies. It will also produce more reverent worship.

Young people's groups should use the chapel for their worship on Sunday nights—and will appreciate it. On Sunday morning they should be in the church service, either in the choir or the pews.

Many women's groups are developing programs of worship which are fresh and meaningful. They could use the chapel for their worship period during their regular meetings, or for special worship services.

In the city most Catholic churches are open during

the day for meditation and prayer, and many of them are used for this purpose by surprising numbers of people. Several hundred can be found at prayer at almost any hour in St. Patrick's Cathedral in New York or St. Peter's Church in Chicago's Loop. Protestants have the same need for quiet meditation. What we have commonly lacked has been a fitting place. In the past, few of our churches would inspire anyone to spontaneous prayer. If a church is located where people are passing by, a chapel which can be easily entered and which is of its very nature inspiring will attract individuals bent on private worship.

The keynote of a chapel should be intimacy. It should accept the individual. This means that the scale should be personal rather than imposing. The room should wrap itself about anyone who enters. The worshiper should feel himself a part of the setting.

A chapel should be readily accessible. People should be able to get in without being looked over by anybody else. This calls for a direct entrance from the outside if possible. It should also be connected with the rest of the building in such a way that church school departments and other groups can come and go without exposing themselves to the weather. If it is to be used for weddings, the chapel should be near a room where receptions can be held.

A chapel should be small. We would suggest a maximum seating capacity of 60 but would prefer something less. This will take care of most groups bent on worship; larger groups should use the church.

Chairs are better suited to chapels than pews. This is traditional, but it is also sound sense. A pew is a cumbersome piece of furniture which goes best in a large room. Chairs are more individual and personal. Chairs also permit greater flexibility in the use of the room. Properly arranged, twenty people can fill the room, while at other times thrice that number can be crowded in.

The style, color scheme, and decorations of a chapel should be the reverse of the church to which it is attached. To add a colonial chapel to a colonial church is silly. Contrast is worth far more than conformity. If the church has a high ceiling, the chapel should have a low one. If the church has clear glass, the chapel should have stained glass. If the church is predominantly white, the chapel should major in the deeper hues. If the church has a red dossal, the chapel should have blue or green.

As we have kept reiterating, the genius of a chapel is intimacy. Everything is close at hand. This invites an elaborateness of decoration which is impossible in most churches. The grain of wood, delicate gradations of color, intricacy of design are lost in a church, but they can be great assets in a chapel. A chapel is rarely occupied for more than thirty minutes at a time. Bright colors and dramatic effects which would become tiresome in a church where people come every week for an hour can be inspiring in a chapel.

Because of its small size and its irregular use a chapel invites venturesomeness. If a mistake is made, it can be remedied at relatively small cost. This is the place to experiment with novel lighting effects, even using color. If somebody wants to paint a mural, why not let him— provided that he agrees that someone else can paint it out if that should become desirable. A chapel is a lovely place for the noble art of woodcarving. Even ceramic decorations can be used. A chapel should be something to play with. It can be far more daring and individualistic than a church.

The very nature of a chapel invites its use for memorials, either as a whole or in its parts. If an individual or a family wish to remember some loved one, here is a chance for them to exercise both their talents and their generosity. They will develop unexpected ideas, spend far more money than they started out to, and have a wonderful time expressing themselves. We know of a church which made its chapel a general memorial for all who wished to share in it. The result was $15,000 in cash and a room which many people felt was peculiarly theirs. Of course there needs to be a coordinating committee both to suggest and to pass on proposed memorials, making certain that they fit into the total scheme of things; but far more liberty can be allowed than is desirable in a church.

Here and there one finds homemade chapels. Sometimes an individual but more often a group of young people lay hold on some unused or little used room in a church and see what they can do with it. They contribute their own efforts, they dig up furnishings from here and there, they levy on their friends for funds to buy what is lacking, and they produce something which is wonderful in their own eyes and a surprise to all comers. There should be more of this sort of thing.

A chapel is not a necessity for most churches, but an elective. It can be a blessing to both those who create and those who use it. This is the part of the building in which there are the fewest rules and the biggest opportunity for self-expression.

Chapter 18

KEEPING THE CONGREGATION COMFORTABLE

MORE people are passing through the doors of our churches every year—and they are staying longer. It is wise strategy to make their stay as pleasant as possible.

One of the encouraging signs of the times is that men are having increasing difficulty in disposing of their hats and coats when they get to church. This means both that there are more men around, and that there is less free space in the pews for their wraps. For this we should rejoice.

Indoors, men find hats and coats highly embarrassing, and their impulse is to get rid of them. Fortunately for church planners, as yet the women feel no such urgency, although it may come in time. As a well-designed home has a coat closet near the door, so should a church have a coat room immediately adjoining its main entrance, and so placed that a newcomer cannot miss it. Similar facilities should be available at the other entrances.

This need creates both a financial and an architectural problem. Such rooms cost money, and if the same one can serve for both Sundays and weekdays the economy is obvious. They also take up space. If a church follows the conventional exterior lines, there will not be much room for a coat room adjoining its main entrance. The real answer is to find new ways of relating the different parts of a church to each other, and this is beginning to be done.

The substitution of the coat hanger on a rod for the old hooks is a great gain both in appearance and in the saving of space. If a coat room is impossible, movable racks can be used during the colder months of the year. They should be to one side of the narthex.

Places for the little children to put their things is also important. The smaller they are, the more they feel that their wraps are a part of them. To pile snow suits and little boots in a heap diminishes the dignity of those who wear them, and invites trouble and even tears when they are to be put on again. If a child can have a place that is distinctly his, he will be happier. An excellent practice is to build a series of little stalls and then label them with either the name of the child or the picture of some familiar animal, so that non-readers can identify their assigned places. This is one way to make three year olds feel that they own the church.

For comfort, human beings need a moderate temperature which is neither too cold nor too hot. The history of church heating suggests the pattern which will probably be followed in the development of church cooling.

Originally churches had no heat. Then sensitive

souls brought footwarmers with them. These were followed by stoves which distributed their warmth most unevenly. Instead of heating the room, they roasted some of the people in it. (This can still be seen in the rural South.) Then came the church furnace, which has always been a temperamental institution. Only in recent years have we had consistently even temperatures in our churches.

Air cooling began with the open window and the hand fan, usually donated by the undertaker. Then in the South came the ceiling fan, which did better in some spots than in others, and sometimes grew melodious.

Americans have become accustomed to even temperatures the year round in their homes, their schools, and their places of business. In the winter they will not go to a church if there's any doubt as to its warmth. Within a few years they will be equally hesitant to go to a church in the summer unless they are sure that it will be comfortably cool. Since summer attendance and summer church activity appear to be increasing, the maintenance of a comfortable temperature during all four seasons will be a necessity in the church of the future.

Heating and cooling are two phases of the same operation and should be planned together. Both begin with adequate insulation which will keep a church warm in winter and cool in summer. It will also keep the decorations from discoloration and diminish the danger of the snow sliding off the roof. The main thrust of heat is up. The degree in which it is escaping heavenward is shown by the visibility of the lath and studding through the plaster, and by the speed with which the snow coasts off the roof.

Although the roof keeps the heat in, it is the side walls that keep the cold out. The fewer the cracks and crevices in the walls, the snugger a building. Here the windows are the problem. Cold air does not get through glass but goes around it. Leaded glass, stained or otherwise, is usually a sieve. Windows that open always have cracks. Ventilating a church with raw air from the outside is a barbaric process which we hope is on the way out. The church of the future will have many and large windows, but these will be of solid glass set in well-calked frames. The result will be more warmth in the winter and more coolness in the summer.

The time to insulate a church is when it is built, although remedial measures can do much for an old structure. From the point of fuel economy, a good quality of insulation is all-important. Because it makes no difference in the appearance of a church, there may be some disposition to save money at this point, but it should be strenuously resisted. Insulation is an emphatic must.

In the past our churches have been ventilated by gravity (the hot air rising and the cold air falling) and by opening windows. In the future the air will be changed by mechanical means, which means a blower. This factor will be a major consideration in planning the heating for a church. The trouble with any system of radiators is that they heat but do not ventilate. They also take up space, discolor walls, and sometimes make unseemly noises at inopportune moments.

Radiant heat is enjoying much favor at present.

Under this system the heating element (steam, hot water, hot air, or an electric element) is buried in the concrete of the floor or hidden in the ceiling panels. It works by direct radiation rather than through the use of air. For crawling babies and people with cold feet it is wonderful. The churches that are using it are happy. But radiant heat implies some form of ventilation. With it the heating and cooling processes are quite separate.

The virtue of forced air is that the same mechanism can both heat and cool a church. This is an improvement over the old hot air furnace at two points. Because the air is pushed mechanically, it can travel horizontally much further than when the only force operating was reverse gravity—the tendency of hot air to rise. Because it is forced, it travels faster and does not require the huge pipes which fill the basements of most old churches and were wonderfully successful in the transmission of sound.

Perimeter heating is now popular. It has been found that if the walls are warm the room is warm. One cold winter's night we saw this demonstrated most dramatically in a new church where the door was covered with canvas and the windows with boards. The air-duct was buried in the concrete of the floor around the sides of the building, with vents at the windows and elsewhere. This combined radiant heat with forced hot air. The building was delightfully warm.

With good insulation the heating authorities state unequivocally that it takes less fuel to maintain a temperature of 55 degrees in a church at all times than it does to expel Jack Frost by whooping up the furnaces on Saturday night. The insurance people report that many church fires start when the janitor has all the drafts open trying to get the heat up—and then goes off to get something to eat. Constant heat in a church is also better for the plumbing, the musical instruments, and the decorations.

The use of oil or natural gas for church heating is bringing many changes. The coal bins are gone, and the big furnace rooms are going, with the boy scouts a frequent beneficiary. Coal dust and ashes have departed. The new heating is compact, clean, and not unattractive. As has been mentioned earlier, there is no particular saving in one central unit as against smaller separate units. Any additional cost for tanks is more than covered by the saving on pipes.

The man who invented the thermostat should be canonized by the churches, as his invention is working wonders in their life. Preparing for a meeting at the church in cold weather was once a formidable task. Now all that is required is that somebody turn the thermostat up half an hour ahead of time. This means that committees can meet, choirs rehearse, people come to see the minister whenever it is most convenient for them. This is one of the factors in the increasing use of our church buildings during the week. Reliable heating plus the closed automobile is making the state of the weather a declining factor in church attendance.

Air conditioning of churches is widespread in the South (where religion is as popular in the summer as in the winter), but it is progressing slowly in the North. Economy demands that even the church which cannot afford to install air-cooling machinery immediately should nevertheless plan for it at the time of building. Cold air requires more room than does hot air; if the same ducts are going to transmit both, the ducts must be larger. Cold air falls, hot air rises; if they are to come through the same openings there must be some provision for pushing one up and the other down. It is possible to pump enough cold air into a place of worship to keep it cool for an hour and a half at much less expense than it would be to maintain this low temperature over a longer period. How much of a church needs to be cooled continuously and how much needs only sporadic relief are questions which call for serious study.

Although we are strongly opposed to church basements, many are still with us and some are still being built. Their worst feature is commonly the stairs leading to them, which are usually dark, difficult, dirty, and unsafe. The basement itself presents the kindred problems of moisture and mustiness. A few basements flood, which is a major calamity, but the more common trouble is the moisture which seeps through the walls. The quantity which gets in is immaterial, probably less than a cupful a week. The difficulty is that it smears the decorations and often disintegrates the plaster, while the moisture in the air produces a moldiness which is disastrous to choir gowns and hard on hymn books, particularly during the summer months. The answer is a better circulation of air. If there is a space between the inside and the outside walls, the moisture which gets through the masonry—and there is practically always some—will simply evaporate. Mustiness can be prevented by either keeping the windows open during the summer or running a fan part of the time. Dehumidifiers are not expensive, but are highly effective in extracting summer-time moisture from the air of a church basement. However, the real answer is not to have a basement.

Cleanliness adds to the comfort of a church. Here people wear their good clothes. Here they bring their friends. A church should inspire respect. To do so it should be clean.

The people who built all but our most recent churches assumed that we would always enjoy an abundance of cheap labor. This was also true of hotels, hospitals, steamships, and circuses. The day when human beings will work for a pittance is over. The church janitors of the past were a remarkable group of men. They could mend anything, and wrought wonders for a very small cash return. Many of them were deeply dedicated to their jobs. Most of them are dead, and the rest will not be with us much longer. In the future the churches will pay much, much more money for much, much less work. Whoever the employer may be, the more a man is paid the less inclined is he to work up a sweat. That seems to be one of the laws of life.

If we are to have churches which are reasonably free from dirt we must build cleanliness into their very structure. This is more effective and much cheaper than hiring cleaners. Nor is it as impossible as it may sound. The departure of the coal burning furnace is a great help, while the sealing up of the windows will keep out the dust of the street. Thanks to the automobile, people arrive at the church with cleaner feet than ever before.

New churches should not only be designed to look clean—they should also be easy to keep clean.

Wherever there are people, there is bound to be litter and with it will be dirt. The easiest way to handle the dirt is to keep it out in the first place. The danger is that it may be tracked in. To avoid this the parking lot should have a hard surface and there should be cement walks from it to the church doors. Having facilities for wraps near the entrances will also help.

The best way to encourage the removal of dirt is to make it conspicuous. Because of their addiction to grays and browns many of our older churches look dirty even when they are clean. On the other hand, nothing encourages cleaning like an unmistakable result. In churches we should keep away from dirty colors and major in bright hues. Also the stronger the lights, the easier is it to see the dirt. A white, light church is simpler to care for than one which suffers from the traditional "dim religious light."

To repeat what has been said several times, well designed and properly placed storage facilities are probably the greatest single help in getting an orderly and a clean appearing church. The easier it is to put things away, the less clutter will there be around. The best encouragement to good housekeeping on the part of both the congregation and the janitor is to provide a handy place for keeping everything as near as possible to where it is to be used. Don't expect tables to be lugged from one end of the building to the other, or church school supplies to be carried upstairs. Good provision for storage cannot be overstressed.

The work of the caretaker should be made as simple and easy as possible. Avoid carpets all in one color, particularly red, for they will show every footprint. Provide him with every convenience—cleaners, mops, buckets, and closets in which to keep them. If there is much lawn, get him a power mower. We know of one church that has a motorized snow shovel for clearing the walks of snow. The more abundant the tools, the more he will find to do with them. He should not be expected to carry chairs and tables but should have trucks and dollies for moving them. We have even seen little carts for the transportation of hymn books.

The position of church custodian should be dignified. When an old-time janitor was asked how he got on with the women so well he replied, "I just put my feelings in neutral and let them push me around." This should no longer be necessary. The new janitor should know to whom he is responsible and just what his responsibilities are. If he is to have assistants, his relation to them should be defined. As far as possible, his work should be kept within reasonable hours. He should be given public recognition from time to time. A good man often enjoys a surprising amount of general popularity. Sometimes the janitor is better liked than the minister.

Those who have the qualities needed for the care of a church oftentimes enjoy the position. It takes a combination of tinkerer and philosopher. A liking for people —including even small boys—is a decided asset.

If a church can provide living quarters for the caretaker and can persuade him to live in them, this can be mutually advantageous. A church benefits in many ways by having someone around all the time to safeguard the property.

Proper toilet facilities add much to the comfort of a church, and have been given altogether too little

Durham, Anderson and Freed, Architects

Photograph by Art Hupy

A massive building gains distinction by tower and cross here. Lighting is achieved in the chancel through skylight and large areas of glass; in the nave by narrow saw-toothed windows; and in parish house by conventional windows. St. James Presbyterian Church, Bellingham, Washington.

Alderman and MacNeish, Architects

The cross and communion table are compelling here. An interesting feature is the "punctured" side walls of the church. Wachogue Community (Congregational) Church, 80 Arville Street, Springfield, Massachusetts.

Hills, Gilbertson and Hayes, Architects

Photograph by Warren Reynolds, Infinity, Inc.

The use of exposed brick walls, laminated wood arches, concealed lights, and the placing of the choir all on one side is wholly modern; and yet the rear-lighted cross and the spacious communion table make the room impressively religious in spirit. First Congregational Church, 1800 West Mill Street, Austin, Minnesota.

Pellerin and Dworski, Architects

This spacious lounge looking out on a garden through a glass wall has proved so popular that the church reports it could use two such rooms. Zion Evangelical and Reformed Church, 70 New Street, Mount Clemens, Michigan.

Alden B. Dow, Architect

Photograph by Myron Johnson

Skylighted lounge opening off the main entrance to the church. First Methodist Church, 114 Jerome Street, Midland, Michigan.

Arland A. Dirlam,
Architect

Photograph by
Paul S. Davis

Great simplicity, much natural light enhance this gracious lounge. Clifton Lutheran Church, Humphrey Avenue at Leicester, Marblehead, Massachusetts.

Hills, Gilbertson and Hayes,
Architects

Photograph by
Warren Reynolds,
Infinity, Inc.

A kitchen with an abundance of sunlight through windows with gay drapes, plenty of artificial illumination, dishwasher, coffee maker, stainless steel sink, and soft seats for the cooks. First Congregational Church, Austin, Minnesota.

T. Norman Mansell, Architect

In striking contrast to the stark simplicity of most new churches is the happy union of modern design with richly symbolic decoration in the chapel of Wittenberg College, Springfield, Ohio.

T. Norman Mansell, Architect

This non-traditional but effective tower gives both unity and impressiveness to the combination chapel and library of Wittenberg College, Springfield, Ohio.

thought. While crowds may come to a church, they stay little more than an hour and have scant need for toilets. On the other hand, there are those who work in a church, while the women often come for the better part of a day and have need for an adequate dressing room. The people who make the most use of church toilets are the very young and the older folk.

Many churches have inadequate sanitary facilities, but once in a while a congregation gets extravagant and overbuilds, usually "to take care of the Conference." Location is more important than number. Church toilets should be handy without being conspicuous. We know of a new parish house where they say, "A man has difficulty taking off his coat without landing in the women's room."

There should be at least one toilet for each sex on the main floor. Somewhere in the building should be a powder room which is large enough and suitably furnished to serve even for the adornment of a bride. If possible there should be a child's toilet easily accessible from the nursery and kindergarten.

While visiting a country church in Michigan I heard much about the "Flamingo Room," particularly from the men. When I found out that this was the women's room, I remarked, "You fellows seem to know a lot about that place." They replied, "We should, because we built it!" And they appeared to have had a grand time doing an imaginative job.

Chapter 19

DESIGNING A CHURCHLIKE CHURCH

"What will it look like?" is the first question most people ask concerning a new church, but it should be the last one to be answered. We have purposely postponed the discussion of the exterior until we completed our consideration of every other aspect of the building. This is as it should be. In the past too many architects have gotten a commission by selling a congregation on a pretty picture of their future place of worship. Then they had to jam the necessary facilities for a church inside the lines of the picture, with many unfortunate results. Poorly placed stairways are one of the signs of a church planned from the outside.

"But we want our new church to look like a church!" is the next statement to be expected, usually expressed with lifted eyebrows and a startled tone of voice. Taken literally, this statement can hardly be challenged. All architects and sensible people are agreed that a house should look like a house, a school like a school, and a church like a church. Any building should reveal its function through its form.

But when people ask that a church look like a church, what they really mean is that it look like some church with which they are already familiar, either by sight or by means of a picture. This is a natural attitude. We always think of the new in terms of the old. That is the only way we can get started. Yet if we stopped at that point there would be no progress. The world moves along as man manages to get from the seen to the unseen. This is the function of the imagination. Nowhere is this faculty more needed than in the planning of a place for the worship of God.

The more we appreciate the patterns for building which have come to us out of the past, the more ready will we be to work out new patterns for our own day. Each of the historic styles of architecture represents a triumph of the human imagination and the spirit of daring. We know the masterpieces which have survived; we do not know the failures, many of which just toppled over. By developing columns and lintels the Greeks managed to get a roof over a sizable room. The Romans wanted light for their interiors and worked out the round arch as a means of getting it without weakening the support of the roof. The builders of the Gothic cathedrals wanted more light for their churches in northern Europe, and so devised the pointed arch. On the other hand, the Moors and then the Spaniards built in lands where there was too much sun, and so they escaped from the heat by reducing the number of windows and putting them in deep recesses. Each style of architecture was a brilliant adaptation of the art of building to the needs of the day. Each is a monument to the venturesome spirit of the men of the past.

Inevitably many people are emotionally attached to these masterpieces—but this should not bind us to these patterns. Our enjoyment in singing about the old oaken bucket that hung in the well does not keep us from getting our water out of a faucet.

The traditional ways of building do not suit present-day needs. Yale, Duke, and the University of Chicago have spent many millions for Gothic architecture. On the outside the effect is generally pleasing. The atmosphere is romantic and far removed from the tobacco and the oil which financed two of these building enterprises. The inside is not so good. The windows, and to a lesser extent the doors, had to be put where the exterior design demanded, with the result—many dark and gloomy rooms. The so-called colonial is a bit more flexible but has a hard time escaping from the conception of windows as just holes in the wall. The Model T was a wonderful car in its day, but I would hate to drive one in present-day traffic. The architecture of the past does not meet the necessities of today.

Probably the most compelling argument against the historic styles is their expense. They were developed in a day when labor was cheap. Many of the old crafts are well-nigh extinct. Few congregations can afford the elaboration of detail which gives many old churches their charm.

At present there is no generally accepted pattern for the exterior of a church. The younger architects and the lay people who have really thought about the matter have turned their backs on the traditional styles. The plain truth is that most modern Gothic is plain fakery —a coating of antiquity over a modern steel frame intended to look old when it isn't. By modern standards this is not even honest.

Yet what is to take its place? The man on the street does not like the so-called "modern" churches. A few of these are freaks developed by somebody who was trying to be smart. The objection to most of the churches built in new ways is simply that we have not gotten used to them. They offer a new idea to those who pass by, and most people do not feel comfortable with new ideas. The interiors have had a better acceptance than have the exteriors, partly because they meet the felt needs of those who enter but also because the people who pass judgment are a more select and thoughtful group than the multitude who damn the outside because it jars some of their preconceived notions as to what a church should be.

A church must have an outside as well as an inside. That outside should have a pleasing, significant form. It should witness for God. How is this to be achieved?

Copying is impossible. The old is objectionable on many grounds, the new does not inspire the desire to imitate. This is most fortunate. Whether we want to or not, those who build churches today are compelled to walk in new paths. This is one of the creative ages of the church. We should share in the process of working out new forms. The way to do this is to allow the new church to develop freely as a means of meeting present and future needs with the means, financial and structural, which are available. The new church should be a growth rather than a creation. It should be the result of the thinking of many people rather than the fruit of somebody's brainstorm. This process is simpler than it sounds. If we will take the various factors in the situation they will give us most of the answer.

The first consideration should be given to the needs of the congregation. This is the reason for building the church. Thus far most of this book has been devoted to the study of those needs. These will not be further rehearsed. We would suggest a way in which these may be visualized externally. A rewarding plan of action is to decide on the approximate size of the rooms needed for the future church—place of worship, parish hall, parlors, offices, etc.—and cut out pieces of paper to scale and then play around with their arrangement so that each can be of the most use to the other. This will help to visualize the problem of the exterior.

The location of a church has much to do with how it should be built. This begins with the part of the country. In Florida the outdoors and the indoors can mingle far more than in Maine. A church on a business street must fight for attention much more than one in a residential section.

A careful study of the site will answer many questions. If this is small and crowded by other buildings, vertical lines must be stressed from necessity; if there is plenty of room, horizontal lines should dominate. On every site there is one spot which is more dominant than any other. Here should be placed the feature which announces to all comers that this is a church. There is another spot which will be the most convenient entrance, usually from the parking lot. If these two focal points are clearly perceived, other features will fall in their proper places.

The materials and ways of building now available is

another factor influencing the appearance of your future church. These are utterly different from those used in the traditional styles of the past.

Where you are has much to do with how you build. As transportation adds much to the cost of building materials, few of them travel far. The basis of most outside walls is usually what is known technically as "aggregate block." They are made out of cinders, volcanic rock, cement, and other materials. The name varies in different areas, with the color ranging from near white to near black with a pink variation available in California. Sometimes these blocks are used for exterior walls, painted or unpainted, but more often a veneer is placed on the outer side. Between the veneer and the block there is a quarter inch of air space, which takes care of any moisture which may get through and also provides insulation for both heat and sound. Usually the outside is of brick, which is a local product. Large bricks are more economical than small ones, as a bricklayer will use anything which he can lift with one hand. In a few portions of the country certain types of stone are cheaper than brick, and give an attractive wall. Careful study should be given to the best material for your particular situation.

Roofs are getting much simpler, and consequently more leakproof. They tend to be either flat or near flat, or quite steep. The laminated wood arch is in much favor wherever height is desired.

One of the great virtues of these new materials from the architectural point of view is their light weight. The churches of the past had thick walls with a multitude of heavy beams supporting the roof. They looked like fortresses dedicated to God. Such construction is no longer necessary. The weight upon the foundations is far less than formerly. Instead of supporting the roof, the walls merely keep out the cold. Light and air are everywhere. Instead of being earthbound, the modern church floats on the ground. Great flexibility can be had. All sorts of possibilities are open to the imaginative builder. He enjoys a freedom which architecture has never known before.

The final factor in shaping the exterior of a church is the one with which we began, "What will it look like?" A church should reflect its funcion in its structure. It is a public building in which people assemble to worship God. This should be obvious to all comers. But a church should also speak to people about God. It should have a message for all who see it. As many, many more people go by a church than ever enter, this silent appeal should not be neglected. We all know churches which by their situation and their grace are an adornment to their community and a means of pointing people toward God.

To use material things to suggest the divine is never easy. Today the task is complicated by the practical needs which a church must meet, the nature and extent of the sites on which it is to be built, the novelty of the materials and type of construction which must be used. The greatest difficulty, however, is to find an architectural language which the man on the street will understand. Never was the population more varied. Our problem is to say something in brick and stone which will register on the mind of the wayfaring man, though a fool. We must silently speak so that he who runs may read. This is a major problem.

At this point the vocabulary of the multitude is exceedingly limited. The cross is the one symbol which is universally accepted, although held in suspicion by some Protestants. Anything pointing upward in an emphatic manner will suggest God. Because of past associations, porticoes and pillars have an ecclesiastical connotation for some. These are the scanty tools with which we must work.

On the other hand, it is only necessary for the exterior to say "church" once provided this is done emphatically. One strong symbol is enough. The multiplication of crosses, the addition of towers, the use of pointed windows add little. Once a building has been marked unmistakably as a church, its other features can be whatever it is natural for them to be to serve their appointed functions. This might be called the economy of emphasis.

The location of a church will decide how this principle can best be applied.

If a church opens off the sidewalk of a busy street, we should not expect people to gaze skyward. Rather should the distinctive features be at eye-level. Here an attractive entrance is most important. The ideal arrangement would be to use glass in such a way that the passer-by could look right in, either upon a friendly narthex, or even upon the worship center of the church itself.

Steeples are the supreme symbol of American Protestantism. Our Puritan forebears threw out every symbol within their churches, and then put above them the loveliest steeples that man has ever known—and a steeple is nothing but symbol. To be effective a steeple must be so placed that it can be seen by many from a distance. It does not belong "where cross the crowded ways of life." Steeples are also expensive to build and costly to maintain. We know churches which must spend on the average $500 a year to keep them repaired and painted. Most congregations cannot afford steeples. Rare is the new church which has both the situation and the means for "a finger pointing towards God."

However, the modifications of the steeple are endless. It can be stepped down to a slender spire or to a vestigial remnant such as the fleche. It can be sawed off and adorned with a cupola—a frequent fate of blown-down steeples. It can be broadened out into a tower and given the appearance of utility with a belfry. Almost instinctively churches crave some sort of a vertical symbol. They want the exterior to give people a lift.

The use of the cross offers both problems and possibilities. We do not like small crosses on the outside any more than on the inside. The cross should never be an incidental feature of any setting; it should either dominate or not be there. We also object to having even large crosses stuck on as a sort of afterthought. A frequent device for making an unchurchlike church look like a church is to erect by its side a pylon and then impose a cross on its side towards the top. To us this seems to be forcing things a bit. In California there is a grocery chain which uses as its emblem a pylon without the cross, while the rural-minded associate it with the International Harvester Company.

We believe that a better plan is to incorporate the cross into the structure of a church. The Cabrini Roman Catholic Church of Minneapolis has the cross growing out of the doorway. This is both impressive and meaningful. A more common answer is to either impose or inset the cross on the exterior of the chancel end of a church. The Lakeside Presbyterian Church of San Francisco does this with glass brick. The Episcopal Church in Menlo Park, California, has a dark cross against a background of blue plaster so arranged that it can be illuminated at night. The church in Silver Lake, Ohio, has a dark cross against a white wooden tower. In other instances the outlines of the cross are imbedded in the brickwork. The variations of this idea are endless.

For most churches we would make a simple suggestion. The best symbol for a church is the church itself. This is both economy and honesty. Height is desirable in any place of worship and can be achieved without too much expense through the use of laminated wood arches. This should be the central feature of the building or buildings. Around it should cluster the other rooms as needed, which should be single story and relatively low; this will accentuate the height of the church proper. The end which has the greatest visibility can be given a distinctly religious touch with some variation of the steeple, an imposed cross, or an alluring doorway. The symbols for the church should be fused with the church itself.

If your new church is to meet the needs of the congregation with any effectiveness, it will be an utterly different sort of a building from any which the people have ever seen before. The danger is that to many of them it may be a disappointment if not a shock. For this reason a large proportion of the congregation should be made familiar with the considerations which have made the new church so different from the old, particularly in its external appearance. Here is a wonderful chance for some education as to the whys and the wherefores. The congregation should think itself into the new pattern which is emerging. If this is done successfully the building committee and the architect will be given a freer hand than might otherwise be the case, and there will be fewer complaints afterwards.

At this point the work of the architect is supremely important. Great is his opportunity if he has creative gifts. His task is to fit together the parts of a puzzle so as to form a coherent and meaningful whole. He must take all the factors which have been discussed in this chapter, study their implications, let them work themselves out as far as they can, and then give the whole unity. He should be given all the relevant facts and then protected against the uninformed, the ignorant, the bull-headed, while he works out a solution.

A new type of church architecture is in process of development which may express the spirit of our day as Gothic did that of the Middle Ages. This can be achieved only as churches are willing to venture down new paths. At this point no one can tell which is a blind alley and which the Highway to Tomorrow. Architects are like other artists in that the dividing line between the genius and the crackpot is very thin. The situation calls for faith and daring. You must build. You cannot build after the old patterns. Something new and different is inevitable. If you accept this situation and work at your problems intelligently, you may emerge with something which will be honest, useful, new, and beautiful. In so doing you will be doing your part in developing the new church architecture.

Chapter **20**

PUTTING MANY MINDS TO WORK

IT TAKES a lot of people to build a church. Many men
of many crafts are required to put up a building. They
can be paid only as a multitude of people give of their
means. Behind the builders and the givers are the
planners—the men and women who enlist the interest
and stir up the enthusiasm that makes a new church
possible.

The larger the number of people who are involved in
the planning of a church and the more deeply they are
involved, the heavier the responsibility which they
assume, the better the result will be.

Several seductive perils are to be avoided.

To have one or two people put up most of the money
is most unfortunate. Inevitably the building will reflect
their ideas rather than the thinking of the congregation. The very name "Memorial" has proved a blight on
many congregations. Undoubtedly when someone of

taste starts out to build a church, he or she can achieve more of certain forms of loveliness than an unaided congregation might conceive, but this beauty is always a bit exotic and unrelated to life. It lacks reality.

Easy money from any source is an exceedingly doubtful blessing, whether it comes from the insurance company after a fire, the disposal of property at a profit, or a legacy. Here the peril is foolish spending. A congregation which had leased its site to an oil company for a filling station was planning to use the $15,000 of advanced rent to move an old building, which wasn't worth $15,000, to a new site. If the people had had to raise the money out of their own pockets, they would not have considered the proposition.

Sometimes matters get into the hands of an all-wise committee too soon. This group assumes that it has been ordained to do the job and that it should not "confuse the people" by letting them in on their discussions. They imagine that matters will go better if everything is kept securely in their hands. In this they are usually quite sincere, but they both take upon themselves a responsibility which may become most burdensome, and they deprive the congregation of an experience which is rightfully theirs.

Occasionally a job is turned over to an architect prematurely and too completely—and there are some architects who want just this. This puts the responsibility where it should not be, and invites needless mistakes. No architect knows everything.

As we will point out shortly, there is a time when a small committee must make the necessary decisions and when the architect should be given a free hand, but that is not in the preliminary stages of a building project.

An inspiring instance of the other extreme is the experience of the Community Church in Greendale, Wisconsin, one of the early housing projects of the federal government not far from Milwaukee. This congregation has built its own church, largely because it had to. They even glued together the wood for their laminated wood arches. They have been fortunate in having an architect who has worked right along with them and who has not been peeved when the crowd overruled him at certain points. The men have had so much fun matching their wits against the various problems which have confronted them that they have become reluctant to contract out anything—they would rather do it themselves. The worst drawback has been the time—two years—it has taken to get the building done. The greatest gain has been the way that the church has become a part of the lives of those who have built it. One of the leaders states: "Wherever these men go and whatever becomes of them, they will always feel that this is their church." When this happens a congregation cannot fail to prosper. Its greatest endowment is life, which is priceless.

The greater the number of people who are enlisted in the planning for a new church, the better the result will be.

A church is a complicated structure which must serve a wide variety of needs. No one committee and certainly no architect can be fully cognizant of all the demands which will be made on the building. Many minds are needed so that nothing be forgotten. Another peril is the weariness which will inevitably overtake the committee and the architect. Two recent comments are significant. The pastor of a church which cost $750,000 says, "The architect just wasn't big enough. He could not get his mind around all the phases of the job." In explaining some of the faults in an even larger building the minister said, "By the time they got to the chapel they were running out of money, energy, and enthusiasm." In neither case are we disposed to put much blame on the architect. The churches involved asked for too much. The more minds there are working on a proposition, the fewer the mistakes which will slip by, and the better the outcome.

The larger the group which has been pondering the problems involved in building a church, the more money will there be available for the solution of those problems. Nothing excites interest like active participation. The more people do for a church the more they will talk about it—and they will inevitably persuade both themselves and their friends into giving more than would otherwise be the case. Widespread sharing in the planning is the best promotion any project can possibly have, and will pay off splendidly in dollars and cents.

The end result will be a stronger congregation. People grow as they carry responsibilities. Those who share in the planning of a new church will appreciate what the building stands for and how it can be used when it is built. As has been pointed out, it will be different from any church the people have previously known, and there will be criticisms and complaints. If a considerable part of the congregation has shared in the thinking that produced the building, they will be only too glad to explain and interpret it to its critics.

To secure this type of participation we urge the appointment of as many committees as possible to explore different angles of the proposition while the plans are still in a preliminary stage. The business of these groups is not to settle anything, but to find out what needs to be known. They are expected to spy out the land and then to report back to the congregation, its governing body, or the committee which has the overall plans in hand. Each committee should be given a real problem on which thought is needed.

Here is where just such a book as this can offer immediate, practical assistance. As has been pointed out, the natural response, when a new building is suggested, is to remember the old, familiar buildings of the past. Real progress can rarely be made until this nostalgia has been eliminated—until constructive thinking has replaced gilded memories. To achieve this, something new must be introduced to displace the old—and, as you must know by now, that is the theme of this book! Moreover, the simultaneous reading of the same book by a number of people gives them a "conversation piece" which provokes profitable discussions. A dozen copies being read by a dozen people at the same time will produce more results than one copy read by the same number of people consecutively. Simultaneous reading produces corporate thought, which is precisely what is needed for the building of a church.

The committee assignments fall into three classifications: (1) Functional, (2) Structural, and (3) Watchdog. The first group is concerned with the various activities which take place in a church; with the ways in which they are related to one another, and—vitally important—how the rooms in which they are carried on can best be related to one another.

Use of Site for Parking Lot and Buildings. This is the first and most fundamental problem and should enlist some of the best brains in the congregation. What is the most conspicuous spot on the site? How may this best be exploited? For how many cars should parking be planned? Where should the entrance from the highway be placed? How should it be marked? Should there be a separate exit? What should be the relation between the parking lot and the main entrance to the church? Where should the small children be left? What space should be kept for future expansion? What provision should be made for those who come on foot? (See Chapter 4.)

The Place of Worship. What should the seating capacity be? Would multiple services be desirable? What is the experience of churches in similar situations that have tried them? Is provision for overflow congregations likely to be necessary? How can this best be arranged? What would a balcony cost? How much would it be used? How effective is it as a place of worship? What are the factors which create the spirit of worship in a church? How can these be achieved? To find the answer it is suggested that other churches be visited and the effect which they create on worshipers studied. (Chapter 6.)

The Arrangements for Music. Is a pipe organ contemplated? How much space should be allowed for it?

How can it be placed so that it can be heard to the best advantage? Where can the console be located so that the organist can hear the instrument as the people hear it, see and hear the choir, and observe the service without being too conspicuous? How large a choir does the church expect to have? How many choirs? How can they be so seated as to be supported by the organ, seen by the organist, and at the same time see the minister and participate in the worship? How much space will they need for music and gowns? Should a place for a Sunday morning "tune up" be provided? How should the choir go from the place of assemblage to the place where they sing? Should a rehearsal room be provided, or can the regular choir loft serve for that purpose? If an electronic organ is to be used, how may the sound boxes be placed so as not to deafen the choir and organist? This committee will find it profitable to visit other churches, asking the people in charge of the music to tell them what is right and what is wrong about their setup. (Chapters 9 and 10.)

Religious Education. What is the present age distribution of the church school? What is it likely to be five years from now? What proportion of the children are brought on foot? in cars? arrive by themselves? Would it be agreeable to the parents to have classes for pre-school children during the church service? What would be the economies in a two-session school? Could all grades be cared for at both hours, or would it be necessary to split the school on an age basis, the younger children coming at one time, the older at the other? If the church provided good nursery and kindergarten rooms would they be used during the week for nursery school or kindergarten? How many classes are run on a discussion basis and would therefore need separate classrooms? Where the emphasis is on activity and notebook work, can several classes meet in the same room? What provision should be made for the use of visual aids? Would a chapel reduce the space needed for departmental assemblies? (Chapter 11.)

Social Facilities. Does the congregation linger after church? How can the social instincts of the people be given a chance to express themselves without jamming the aisles or pushing folks out on the sidewalk? Would a "coffee hour" be desirable? What social functions should the church provide for? What is the local practice concerning the size of weddings? the place for receptions? To what extent do the women's groups meet at the church? How many dinners will the church normally have in the course of a year? How large will they be? Will there be a program following? Do the young people need a homey place in which to meet? Would an attractive parlor be used by outside organizations? What types of indoor recreation are popular in your community? What sort of space would they require if they are to be carried on in the church? (Chapters 12 and 13.)

Food Service. This committee should work closely with the one on Social Activities. What should be the maximum number of people to be served at one time? What is the proper proportion between dining space and kitchen space? What are the local sanitary requirements for public eating places? What provision should be made for the storage of food? How much baking is there likely to be at the church? What are the conditions which make it easy to serve small lunches and dinners? What provisions should be made for light refreshments? If there is to be a kitchenette, how small should it be? This committee needs to visit other churches to enquire how their facilities work. They can also learn something from the experience of the schools, which serve simultaneous meals. Often the Home Bureau or the state university extension can be most helpful. (Chapter 14.)

A second group of assignments has to do with building methods. Ultimately, of course, this is the responsibility of the architect, yet the congregation will profit from its own studies of the subject in two ways. The more a congregation knows about technical matters, first of all, the more intelligently it can consider the proposals of the architect and deal with subcontractors and suppliers. Second, the studies will make the whole project more vivid and inspiring to the knowledgeable laymen, who will take added delight from working on these committees simply because they are dealing with familiar matters.

Ways of Building. What materials are most used locally? Does your climate call for special care at any point? Is the soil of your site such that a concrete slab floor can be laid right on the ground? What are the angles of the sun, particularly in December and January? What is your rainfall? What is the relative cost of a flat roof? a shed roof? one supported by laminated wood arches? This committee can learn much by looking at new school houses, particularly when they are in process of construction. It should get at the facts as to the relative cost of one story as against multi-story buildings. It should help the architect to interpret the newer ways of building to the congregation. (Chapter 2.)

Heating. This has been revolutionized in recent years, with many people still thinking in old terms. What is the most available fuel in your community? How may it best be used? How much thought should be given to either the present or future introduction of air conditioning? Will one central heating unit or several scattered ones be more economical? more desirable? How may the various rooms be best insulated? How can doors and windows be made tight? What height of ceiling will be needed for effective ventilation? Can the necessity of opening windows be avoided? What are the merits of radiant heat? How does its cost compare with other methods? (Chapter 18.)

Lighting. Here, again, a new day has dawned. A study should be made of the lighting used in the better schools, banks, stores. Often a visit to the local funeral establishment will be helpful. Careful consideration should be made of the different types of lighting needed in the entryway, the social areas, the church proper, where church school pupils do notebook work, the kitchen, corridors. Every effort should be made to tailor the lighting to the need. Instead of using one system throughout the church, there should be the maximum different types of light. This will not happen unless somebody works on it. (Chapter 7.)

Sound Control. Where should sound-absorbent materials be used? Where should sound be magnified, and how? Should there be a public address system? (See Chapter 9.)

The third group of assignments is for a longer period

of time. As the planning for a church proceeds, there is a danger that certain needs will be pushed to one side and forgotten. Building committees and architects grow weary with the multiplicity of their tasks. Unless certain concerns are protected by special pleaders, they are likely to be overlooked. These assignments call for imaginative, persistent people who will first inform themselves as to what is needed and then insist that these needs be cared for.

Storage. This should be a watchdog committee with its eye on everything. It should have a long life, although not necessarily a happy one. This is the place for strong-minded people. They should keep asking, "Where are you going to put it?" They might well begin with the hats and coats which men wear to church, but they should not overlook the rubbers and snow suits which the kiddies wear. They should prowl about until they are experts on coat racks of all kinds, storage walls, cabinets, trucks and dollies on which chairs and tables can ride about, janitors' closets, even garbage disposal. Good storage facilities will enhance the usability of a church by nearly fifty per cent, and the only way that it can be achieved is by eternal watchfulness on somebody's part. (Chapter 18.)

Toilet Facilities. These must not be left to chance, as this is one of the places where the building committee and the architect often get tired. What are the state requirements? How can the small children best be provided for? The older people? Do the women need a dressing room? What provisions should be made for brides? (Chapter 18.)

Landscaping and Greenery. Although this may come

last in point of time, it needs to be planned from the beginning. How can the entrance to the parking lot be made attractive without blocking the view? How can the lot itself be given a setting which will promote eye appeal? What plantings should there be about the outside of the church? What provision should be made for greenery on the inside? How can growing things add to the effectiveness of the place of worship? The social areas? Should the urns and boxes be built in? How related to the windows?

Furnishings. Because these are among the last things to be decided, this is another area where the responsible parties grow weary, which makes them susceptible to the wiles of the salesman. In the past most churches have been oversold on pews. We know a church where the good women wanted to do what was right, so they bought everything the salesman had to offer by way of chancel furniture, and the result was a confusing clutter. What is needed is a group which will give these matters a long-time study so as to have good suggestions ready when the order is finally placed. They should consider the various types of pews both from the angle of comfort and appearance. (Square top pews will increase the apparent depth of a church.) They should cooperate with the architect in the design of the chancel furniture. Here two factors are important; simplicity, and sufficient contrast so that the communion table and the cross may command attention. Accessories should be held to a minimum, and the people discouraged who want everything to match.

The less money a congregation has to spend, the

more necessary is this process. To the wealthy congregations mistakes may be just an incident; to a poor congregation they are calamities. Careful thought is the secret of true economy. Incidentally, we have found the most difficult congregations to deal with those that thought they had plenty of money. They assume that they can buy what they want, but it is not that simple. Poverty can be a marvelous stimulus to mental activity, and no set of plans ever suffered from too much of that.

Church officers hesitate to invite the congregation to share in the planning because they fear that it will "divide the church" and because they are afraid of the fools.

This peril is very real if the people are allowed to vote on matters about which they are poorly informed. In that case opinions will be based on preconceived notions, old prejudices, and pure emotion, because this is all that they have to go on. The whole purpose of the course we have suggested is to get the people to face the facts. If one committee has done a good job of investigating, it will assume that the others have done the same and will be inclined to accept their findings. The thinking of the group will be based less on personal opinion and more on objective fact. On this basis, divisions are unlikely.

The fools are those who acquired an idea, usually a long time ago, and who are loath to part with it. The extent to which they are a nuisance depends upon how closely real knowledge of the situation is limited. If one or two people shout down a fool, the crowd will sympathize with him. The larger the number of those who have had some share in reaching decisions, the easier it is to take care of the opinionated dissenter. The crowd will squelch him.

Not free discussion, but the lack of it, disrupts the peace and unity of a congregation. The peril lies in too many decisions being made by too few people. Most churches resent having their thinking done for them—even when it is good thinking.

What effect will the findings of these committees have upon the work of the architect? For the most part they will be helpful. The bane of the architect is the client who does not know his own mind. Most of the difficulties church members have with architects spring from their own muddle-headedness. The more clearly a congregation has thought through its problems, the easier does it become for the architect to formulate his solutions.

In all probability there will be points where the people and the architect will not agree. This is likely to happen in any case. A difference of opinion based upon fact is much easier to work out than one based on prejudice or emotion. The larger the number of people who really think about the matters involved in planning a church, the greater will be their sympathetic understanding of the architect. They will appreciate what he is trying to do and will have some notion of what he has to contend with. Entire agreement between architect and congregation is not to be expected nor desired. What is profitable to both is intelligent differences, from which each is likely to learn. A congregation can have too many fixed ideas, but it cannot know too much about the project which it is undertaking.

Building a new church, or re-building an old one, is a venturesome undertaking. The first requirement is courage, or faith, if you will. The risk of dollars is inevitable. Success will depend very largely on how far the minds of the people are involved. Unless they do a lot of thinking both their daring and their giving may be futile.

Chapter 21

ASKING FOR MONEY CAN BE FUN

THE best time to ask for money is when the largest number of people are most interested in building a church.

If the committee assignments are made as suggested in Chapter 20, and the people work at their jobs, there should be an increasing crescendo of discussion throughout the parish for two, three, or four months. This can be accentuated by having the committees meet on the same night to report their findings to one another. Reports should be made by the committees to the general committee, to the governing body of the church, and to the congregation. These reports may be circulated, or the whole matter can be brought to a head with a parish dinner at which the various groups report. The aim should be to achieve the maximum amount of talk without letting plans jell in such a way that some are for, and others set against them.

Some will always argue, "The people will not give unless we show them exactly what we are going to build. We must have something definite to sell." Some money-raising organizations take the same position. It's just not true.

A congregation should know what it wants and have a clear notion of the direction in which it is moving before it launches a financial campaign. No one questions this—and the preceding pages have shown how this can be done. Yet the record of the churches that have gone to their people on the basis of a real need and a lively dream is astonishing. The First Parish Church in Brunswick, Maine, raised $70,000 for an educational building without deciding which side of the street it would be on. The Methodist Church in Bellevue, Ohio, went out after $54,000 and raised $83,000, and the only tangible thing they had to offer was an option on some land. The Methodist Church in Oxford, Massachusetts, with an annual budget of $15,-000, pledged $105,000, in spite of the fact that in the middle of the campaign they discovered that they could not get the site on which they had set their hearts.

People will give more liberally for a church that they have dreamed about than for one which has been worked out in detail on a blueprint. Psychologists tell us that we respond better to an appeal to the imagination than to the call of duty. A poem stirs us more than a sermon.

There are several practical advantages to postponing the elaboration of detailed plans until after the financial appeal.

The people will give best on the basis of ultimate objectives. A church building should never be an end in itself. In one sense it is merely the outer garment of the church. It is a means towards bringing the Christian gospel to bear upon human lives. The more we put the emphasis at this point, the larger will be the response.

No one can quarrel with these larger purposes. On them the people can all unite, while just as soon as we get into the details of the future structure there are bound to be differences of opinion. Once an elderly woman asked what had been served at a dinner, and she was given the complete menu. "I would not like that dinner," was her comment. "Why?" she was asked. "Because they served olives, and I don't like olives!" she replied. When detailed plans are presented to a congregation there will always be some around who "don't like olives."

A plan that is still fluid permits a more persuasive approach to the givers than one which has been worked out in detail. It is one thing to go to a person with the plea: "This is what we are going to do; how much will you give us?" It is far better tactics to say, "This is what we want to do; if you give us a thousand dollars we will build that much more church!" Givers do not like to feel that they are just tossing their dollars into a pot; they are better pleased if they know that their gift will make a perceptible difference in what is done. On this basis the man who asks for the money is also likely to be more persuasive. He is doing more than collecting dollars, he is adding something to the future church.

This is also an honest approach, and one with which the faint-hearted cannot quarrel. No congregation knows what it can do until it has found out what its resources are. Instead of saying "This is what we will build; let's go get the money," there will be less complaint from the cautious if the sales talk is, "Here is what we want; now we must find out how much we can raise toward it." Few can object to a campaign on this basis. It really puts the proposition up to the people. They decide by their pledges what will be done.

Delaying the detailed plans until after the financing is also sound economy. The place where the most congregations have wasted the most money is in having their plans drawn too soon. If any time elapses between the preparation of the drawings and their execution, there will be changes, and these changes will cost money. What often happens is that the original layout proves to be too ambitious—or the price goes up in the meantime. This means cutting here and changing there. One result is that you are not going to give the people what you promised them when you asked for their money. Another result is that there is danger that these reductions may be made in haste and carelessly and may result in a mess. For instance, a large church had to revise its plans several times. When the building was finished the acoustics proved to be bad. For the original plans they had been figured correctly, but the changes threw them out of scale. Fortunately an acoustical engineer was able to correct the situation at an expense of only $500. This is precisely the sort of thing that happens when the cost of a building must be scaled down. It is far more economical to find out what your resources are in the first place and then plan within those limits.

If ten or a dozen committees have been really working they will also have done a lot of talking and their friends and neighbors will be tolerably well-informed as to what is afoot. This will prevent the campaign from being launched in a vacuum. In one instance a church based its appeal on a statement of its needs as presented in a brochure by the chairman of the trustees, the president of the women, the superintendent of the church school, the leaders of the youth groups. Each appeal was supplemented by pictures showing the present crowding. This was most convincing.

If the people insist on having something to look at, keep it tentative. A good tactic is to print pictures of what other churches have done, with the statement that something similar to this is contemplated. If something more definite is demanded, hire an architect to draw a pretty picture and possibly a floor plan, but make it clear that this is suggestive rather than definitive of what may be built. It is important that the architect be paid for his work. He will offer to do it for nothing, or to charge it off against his fee when he gets the job, but such gifts are to be resisted as they commit the church to hiring that architect. For a church to tie its hands in this way so as to save a few dollars has frequently proved most unfortunate.

As the plans for the new church begin to jell the inevitable question is, "How much money can we spend?" The answer is, "More than you think—particularly if the planning arrangements which we have outlined are being followed." The primary factor in all giving is interest. People will pay for that which they want. Here, again, we favor an experimental approach. Instead of setting a goal and then working up the interest with which to meet it, it is better to let the interest develop to the point where the goal sets itself. In the earlier stages of a building project the dollar sign should be kept in the background.

The men who make a business of conducting church building fund campaigns have several formulas for estimating the giving capacity of a congregation. The professionals claim that they can raise from five to seven times the current giving over a period of three years for a major project. For a two-year campaign some denominational officials claim that they can raise from three to four times the annual giving, while on a one-year basis, double the budget is a figure to shoot at. Here a curious factor comes into the situation. The more campaigns a church has been through, the more it can raise, while the church that has gone for thirty or more years without making a major financial effort is the most difficult one to handle. The more a church has given, the more it can give.

But giving is only part of the picture. For a building project a church should also borrow, either from the denomination or some lending agency. Here the memories of the Depression are often a deterrent, when some churches were lost by foreclosure, more defaulted and had to scale down their debts, and many more went through dark and troublous times paying even the interest on their mortgages. We do not believe that this experience will be repeated. Most of the churches which got into difficulties were built foolishly. Some congregations expected the next generation to pay for the pretentious structures which they were bequeathing to them. Others built for the glory of impressing their neighbors. Gymnasiums, which were expected to bring in the people—only didn't—added to their debts and their difficulties. We know of only one church which had built tastefully and sanely which went down to defeat, and it was overwhelmed by an alien migration. Today denominational officials are very watchful at this point and discourage congregations from borrowing more than they can easily pay. Two formulas have been developed for judging this amount: three and a half times the annual budget, or $200 per family.

Putting these computations together, if your church has a budget of $12,000 and 200 families, it should be able to raise $60,000 and borrow $40,000—and this would be on the conservative side.

"How do we get the money?" is the next question. Although there are various ways of conducting a campaign, which we will discuss later, the underlying principles in any money-raising effort are essentially the same.

The people must be told what the objectives are. All are agreed that word-of-mouth publicity is the most effective. People are most deeply influenced by what they hear from their friends and neighbors, as every politician knows. The methods which we are advocating will have their maximum effectiveness at this point.

But it is also necessary that the eye confirm what the ear has heard. For many the printed page has much authority. In any large congregation are those who can be reached in no other way. It is also important that the same word gets to everybody at the same time. The first step in a financial campaign is to prepare an attractive, convincing statement of what is proposed to be done and to distribute it widely to the constituency.

This should be followed by one or more letters giving the details as to when the calls will be made, etc. One may be written by the minister, the other by a layman. As far as the public is concerned, this is the groundwork of the campaign.

The next step is to recruit the men who will do the work of asking for the money. Usually these recruits are all men. It has been found that this is a job which men will do, if the responsibility is wholly on them. There should be sufficient workers so that they can go two by two and so that the constituency can be covered with not more than eight calls assigned to any team. In some churches, particularly in the smaller communities, getting sufficient manpower may be the crucial problem. Part of the solution is the setting up of the preliminary committees which we have suggested. Those who have shared in the planning will be the most ready and willing to ask for the money.

The third phase in the preparation is the training of the canvassers. This is the heart of the whole matter. To send men out just to ask for money is to invite failure. They will go reluctantly, they will speak hesitantly, and their lack of confidence will be reflected in the pledges they receive. With training, these same men will go forth cheerfully, expectantly, and will get the money. If they know what they are to do, most men will do it effectively. Some campaign directors ask the canvassers to meet for four nights for training. This seems like a lot of time, but it is needed if laymen are to be introduced to a whole set of new ideas in such a way that they can use them persuasively.

The objectives of the campaign must be formulated.

The canvassers should have a sufficient knowledge of the details of the situation to be able to answer questions intelligently; but they need to be taught to state their case on the ultimate objective, which is the presentation of the Christian gospel to people of all ages together with the effective training of the young. The stronger the emphasis at this point, the greater will be the success.

The men need some training in salesmanship—to enter with confidence, to state the reason for the visit immediately, to avoid arguments, to stick to the matter in hand, to stay as long as is necessary, but also to get on to the next place when their mission is accomplished. There should be some discussion of how to handle different types of people. A grouch can really be a wonderful prospect, if dealt with properly.

The most difficult but in some ways the most fundamental part of the training is in the motivation for giving. The principles of stewardship need thorough discussion. Each of us has a certain amount of money passing through our pockets which is not predestined for the tax collector or the grocery store and which we can spend pretty much as we please. Does the way we handle this part of our income reflect our deepest desires, our real convictions, or is it being frittered away in response to the wiles of the advertising geniuses? How much does my budget reflect me! That is a question with which laymen can have a lot of fun.

Only as the men are trained to it will they use a religious appeal. They must be convinced of its relevance and power, and also be assured that the other fellows are also using it. Here group psychology is most important. This religious approach can be put in two ways. One school of thought holds that we should give because we love God; another school has it that if only we can be persuaded to give with sufficient generosity, we will learn to love God. Either way, giving and our attitude towards God are closely related. The deeper we get into a man's pocket, the more likely are we to evangelize him. The more the canvassers face these matters, the better job they will do.

If these preliminary steps are taken effectively, the success of the canvass is assured. The people know what they are to be asked to give for; the men know how they are to present their case. In this situation there is no room for embarrassment and little chance for failure.

But how can this preparation best be achieved?

Some will argue that their church is competent to do this for itself. There are no secrets about money raising, and no real shortcuts. Why don't we just do it? This sounds plausible. Occasionally a church has a sufficiently forceful and dedicated lay leadership to handle a financial campaign. A few churches have been through so many efforts that they have the habit. But most churches need outside help, particularly in the training of the workers. This is something which the minister cannot do, nor can neighboring pastors be imported for the job. The man who tells the visitors how to go about their job must come from afar, and must speak with undoubted authority.

Occasionally a canvass is directed by remote control. A church is given full directions, supplemented by a visit or two or frequent phone calls, and then put on its own. This arrangement helps to keep a congregation on schedule. It follows a definite plan. It has worked well in some instances, particularly for moderate goals.

Several denominations have money raisers on their staffs. These are available to the churches for one or two week periods at a cost of $200-$500 and entertainment. These men assume that the publicity and the recruiting have been largely done before they get there. They major in the training of the canvassers and in the appeal which is made on the canvass Sunday. Their success, too, depends largely on what has been done before their arrival.

Then there are the organizations which make a business of conducting church financial campaigns. They do not work on a commission basis, but for a flat fee, which is a diminishing proportion of the total as the objective rises. The time their representative spends on the field depends upon the size of the fund to be raised, and he may be given a helper if that is necessary. The director of the canvass does not solicit directly. His function is to see that the congregation does the things which need to be done at the time that they should be done. The congregation pays to be persecuted into doing its duty, but most of them regard this as a very good investment. The situation is one of confidence. After an unusually successful campaign, one minister said, "I can pick holes in their procedures at several points, but they achieved the one thing that was needful—they convinced the church that it could do this job." From Maine comes this choice testimony, "We're paying a lot of money for that fellow, and if we do not do what he tells us to we won't get our money's worth."

Quite often it is my privilege to visit a church in the wake of a financial canvass, and I have never known a congregation that did not profit in a number of ways. Rarely if ever has there been any grief. One canvass director made a forthright statement: "In any cooperative effort some animosities may develop. It is best to have them directed toward me rather than some local person, because I can take them out of town with me!"

A building fund campaign helps the current expense budget. Here is an interesting testimony. "We combined our local support and our building fund canvass, asking people to merely renew their current expense pledge, with all the emphasis on the building fund. On this basis we pledged a bit less than the previous year, but we have been taking in more money. What has happened is that the people pledged so heavily for the building fund that they do not dare get behind for even a week, and this regularity of payment has carried over to church support."

We do people good as we teach them to give. A building ups their sights.

Chapter 22

AT LONG LAST WE BUILD!

CHURCHES are long-lived, slow-moving institutions. To lead a congregation out of a doubtful, hesitant frame of mind—and thus into a new building!—usually takes years. Impatience is one of the major perils threatening this process. People "want to see something happen." But haste may work against a building venture in two ways. When nothing seems to be taking place, some eager souls will assume that they have been defeated; but this may be far from true. Or, in their desire to get things moving, they may make premature decisions which can prove most costly. Too many churches are in too big a hurry to build to do it as wisely as they should. Three months, six months, a year does not mean much in the life of a church; yet a mistake made by a hasty committee can blight the congregation for years. One of the purposes of this book is to bring to the attention of churches the many, many factors involved in any building project.

The task requires time. It took the Christian Church in Lakewood, Ohio, five years to plan and build their place of worship. "We were poor," one of their laymen explained, "and we needed all that time to raise the money." Yet the building committee managed matters so that there never was any sense of defeat or undue delay. They did this by keeping the congregation continuously informed as to what they were doing. Every week or so they reported on one thing or another, and apparently the congregation never had a dull moment. The more the spotlight of publicity plays on every step of a building venture, the better the end result will be.

At the conclusion of its financial campaign a church will have a considerable amount of cash and a larger sum in pledges. At this time someone should approach the denominational authorities to see what may be expected at a later date in the way of a grant and loan and what the terms will be. If the denomination is not prepared to help, or if their aid promises to be insufficient, the local bank should be sounded out as to what it might lend to the church. This should not be done until after the canvass, as the amount raised will have a direct bearing on what can be borrowed. The more the people give, the more will the denomination or the bank be prepared to risk. Of course final commitment on their part should not be expected at this time. What the church needs is some knowledge of what it can expect. The pledges plus the cash on hand plus the prospective loan will set the financial limits of the undertaking.

If the church has followed the course we have outlined, it will have the reports of a number of committees on various aspects of the proposed building. These will have been discussed by the committees and church officers and will have been unofficially reviewed by the congregation at the time of the canvass. Out of all this talk there should have emerged a general picture of what can be done and also of what the congregation wants done.

At this point either the congregation or the governing body of the church should pass a vote authorizing further action. This should state the extent of the building to be undertaken, establish the limits of financial expenditure, and place responsibility for the carrying through of the project.

As the emphasis shifts from thought to action the number of people who make the detailed decisions will become steadily smaller. In theory, at least, the desires of the congregation and the findings of the various committees should funnel through a smaller and smaller group as they are carried out. The people who make the final, detailed decisions should do this in the light of all that has been thought and discovered by the congregation. Most of the exploratory committees should also stand by to criticize the plans as they develop, while some of the committees will have their period of greatest activity while the blueprints are being made and even while the construction is under way.

An active building committee should not number more than eighteen or twenty people. Almost inevitably it will consist largely of those who have had a part in the preliminary investigations. Its first job should be to take the various proposals and jell them into a consistent whole. It should not draw detailed plans, but it should decide what plans should be prepared for— how large a church, what other rooms, the general layout, some thoughts as to the way of building. To use an architectural term, they should "state their problem."

This is the point at which an architect should be definitely engaged and put to work. In the preliminary stages he should be consulted on particular problems. Before the congregation purchases a site, an architect should be asked to look at it and should be paid for his time and trouble. Some of the exploratory committees should talk to architects. Usually the architect will save himself time and trouble and the church will save confusion and money if he is not employed until the church knows what it wants.

On the other hand, many architects like to sign up a church as early as possible. This is partly to make sure that some other architect does not get the job, but also to keep the church from developing impractical ideas and going off on foolish tangents. We do not believe that there is much danger of this if a considerable number of people have been enlisted in the study which we have suggested.

Before selecting an architect a building committee should clearly understand his functions. His task is to take the general conception which the congregation has thought out and give it form and substance and, if possible, to exercise creative imagination in the process. A church does not want an architect who meekly does what everybody tells him to do. We know of one instance of an architect so pliant that after everyone's whims had been added to the plans, the cost mounted to twice what the church could pay. Neither does a church want a man who will simply impose his ideas on the congregation. A church is not built for the glory of an architect but for the use of the people. There should be a lively but friendly interplay between the desires of the congregation and the ideas of the architect. Neither should be bull-headed, but the church should expect the architect to be a bit venturesome. As one layman put it, "There are two kinds of architects: copyists and creators." You want the latter variety.

How can such a man be found? That depends somewhat upon where your church is located and how much money you can afford to spend.

Most congregations begin by looking for a "church architect." However, the American Institute of Architects discourages such specialization. They claim that a competent architect should be able to plan any sort of a building, particularly if he will work with a consultant in that field. An architect who is a good churchman and who delights in building churches substantiates this position: "If I built only churches, I would not bring to each problem the freshness which I now get from doing other buildings as well." In this country there is perhaps a score of firms that do little except churches, and most of these are concentrated in Boston, Philadelphia, Chicago, and Minneapolis. Obviously they can take care of only a fraction of the churches being built. If you are planning a large structure, and can afford it, a good arrangement is to employ one of these men in cooperation with a local architect. This need not increase the total cost, while the wide experience of the man from afar can be supplemented by the knowledge of local conditions of the man on the spot.

There are also several hundred firms that have done some churches, and it is from this group that you are most likely to find your architect. However, the man without church experience should not be wholly ruled out. If you are building church school facilities or a parish house, the pattern will be very close to that of the schools, and a man with experience in this field might be most acceptable. And of course every architect must have his first church. Knowledge of church life is rather essential, as is real ability. We know of one instance in which a competent building committee worked with an architect without previous church experience with a most happy result.

The first test of an architect is what he has done. If he has built several churches and they all look alike you do not want him, but if each appears to be a new creation designed to meet specific needs, that is a strong argument in a man's favor. Some inquiry should also be made as to how the congregation feels about his work.

Often a committee will interview several architects before making a choice. It is a good idea to take them to the site and see how hard they study it. One church chose the man who gave it the most intensive look. They should also be listened to, but it should be remembered that what you want from an architect is not salesmanship or a good speech, but planning ability. What he can do with his pencil is more important than what he can do with his tongue.

A committee must work intimately with the architect it selects. As with a psychiatrist, it is important that they like each other. If either gets on the nerves of the other, the results can be unpleasant if not disastrous. It was said of one architect, "Even when he came up with a good idea, the committee would not take it."

An architect should be properly compensated. He needs to know more than mortal man can know about all sorts of things. He has had a long and expensive training. His tasks require endless patience. He is usually very much of a gentleman.

Bargain hunting is likely to prove disastrous. We know a church which secured complete working drawings for an $80,000 building for the ridiculous sum of $900. The draftsmanship was excellent and they looked fine, but practically everything about them was wrong. When an architect is willing to cut his price it is usually because he is short of work, and there may be good reasons for that fact. It is also well to beware of too much profession of piety. We knew a man who felt he had a "call" to build churches—only the designs which he proposed for a church in the open country and for one in a city were just the same!

The better architects will ask a larger fee for designing a church than for other work, and they are entitled to it. Because one must deal with a committee rather than a single client, churches will consume more of an architect's time—and patience—than other projects. The work itself is also more taxing simply because every feature of a church must be worked out from scratch. A factory, a hotel, a hospital, a school repeat certain features. Homes differ, but an architect does many of them. Churches come less frequently and each is different from every other, and none of the parts repeat themselves. If an architect has an abundance of work, he will not take a church unless paid a premium above the usual fee. That is, if commercial work pays six percent, churches should pay eight. And on top of this the design of furniture and remodelings should have a further premium simply because the labor involved for the architect is out of proportion to the cost of the other work involved.

The fee which the architect gets is divided into three parts.

For the initial surveys and studies and preliminary drawings he receives a quarter of his fee. He is expected to keep on making drawings and floor plans until the committee is satisfied. The more clearly a church has thought through its problems and the more definitely it knows what it wants, the less time and effort will be required on this phase of the work—and the better for all concerned.

For the working drawings and the detailed specifications the architect receives half of his total fee. This is the phase of a job which requires the most of him in the way of expense and effort. Draftsmen are paid real money, and quite a lot of it. This is also the point where architects and churches most often get into trouble. The danger is that the final drawings may be made too soon. What happens is that the committee feels that it is reasonably well satisfied with the preliminary plans but wants to know what they will cost, so someone gives the order to go ahead, complete the plans, and get some bids. These sometimes come in for much more than was anticipated and the result is both financial and personal trouble. We know churches which have paid $8,000 and even $11,500 for plans which were then discarded. This is not necessary. A contractor can take floor plans and a projection and give a reasonably close estimate as to the cost, and it is worth paying him well to do this. Many architects are unduly optimistic when it comes to estimating their costs. One denominational board adds thirty percent to the architect's figures and finds that this usually works out. The architect should not be directed to make working drawings until (1) every reasonable question has been answered, (2) the preliminary plans have been approved by the denominational authorities, where that is required, and (3) the church is satisfied that the cost will be within its means. Here, again, real economy lies in thinking before you act. Corrections in the pencil sketches are easy; in final plans most expensive. A committee should check and double check and then check again before it gives the go ahead signal on working drawings.

Another factor in the situation is the state. A church is a public building and as such is subject to regulation by the state authorities rather than the local officials. The usual requirement is that the plans must be approved by the state fire marshal. Instead of abiding by this rule at the last moment and in a perfunctory manner, a church will profit by seeking the cooperation of the proper authorities from the beginning. This will often save money and is certain to result in a better building. A church is built to stand for at least 50 years. During that time safety requirements are certain to be stiffened. The sensible thing is to anticipate future regulations rather than just get by on the present ones. This is especially true of the rooms used for the children. Most states now discourage the erection of schools with rooms in the basement large enough to accommodate a class. As yet this requirement is not made of churches, but they should be in honor bound to abide by it. If a church will seek the counsel of the state authorities it will find them generally both reasonable and helpful.

The third part of the architect's fee is for the interpretation of the plans and the supervision of the actual construction. Here the churches often expect too much. An architect cannot afford to watch every brick and door put in place. He is supposed to pass on the competency of the workmen, settle the questions which are bound to arise concerning the meaning of the plans, inspect the work as it is done, and certify the proper payment to the contractors.

The amount and quality of the supervision a church will get depends in part upon where the architect lives and in part upon his disposition. Architects take two attitudes towards supervision. Some claim that their conceptions cannot be properly carried out unless they watch every step in the process. Others regard supervision as something of a nuisance. When the architect comes from a distance, arrangements can often be made for some local person to take care of this final phase of the work.

It pays a church to play fair with the architect. It always suffers if he loses money on a job, while it gains when he makes a reasonable profit.

An architect should not be asked to do the impossible. It is proper to say to him, "This is what we want; what will it cost?" or "We have this much money;

how much church can we get?" but it is wrong to sew up both ends of the proposition and say "Give us this church for that amount of money," when it can't be done. Nothing but trouble results when this is tried.

The architect and the building committee are workers together on a common task, but the committee is the senior partner. It pays the bills and carries the ultimate responsibility. The relationship is similar to that of the captain of a ship and the pilot. The latter takes the wheel and guides the ship into the harbor, but the captain stands at his side every foot of the way. If he judges the pilot to be drunk, unwise, or incompetent, the captain takes over the wheel.

A poor architect with a good committee may achieve a better result than a good architect with a poor committee. Once the same architect built two churches in the same city at the same time. One is a gem and the other is a mess. In the first instance the committee was competent and the pastor in control of the situation; in the second the committee was ignorant and bullheaded and the pastor was on the way out. On the other hand, if the committee has thought through its job, it will get out of the architect all that he has to give. Human relations are always important.

The choice of a contractor is second only to the selection of an architect in its importance. No law compels a church to take the lowest bid; rather should it seek out the best man for the job. He can be discovered by looking at the buildings he has put up and by talking with their owners. Many contractors are conscientious and devoted men who take great pride in their work. What they have done for some churches should get them a pass through the gates of heaven. No contract is airtight. A church should choose a builder in whom it has the utmost confidence.

When actual construction starts a rigid chain of command should be established. It should be utterly impossible for last minute brain storms to occur—such as the church which decided to make the basement ceiling a foot higher, but which failed to adjust the stairs! One person and only one person should be authorized to talk to the architect and the contractor. He should listen to both the complaints of the congregation and the problems of the workers, and then decide what to do about them.

When work gets underway a "hoverer" can be a great blessing. This is someone who camps on the job with his eyes open. Sometimes a man who has retired will take the task, usually for love. The fact that he is there all the time prevents many things from going amiss. He learns much, has a good time, and the church benefits by his watchfulness.

The building of a church is about the finest adventure upon which a group of people can embark. It starts as a dream. It progresses as people are willing to dedicate themselves to an ideal. It involves organization, finance, a multitude of mechanical problems. Somewhere along the line nearly everybody can share significantly in the undertaking. Every church stands as a monument to the cooperation of a multitude of people. Yet it belongs to no one. Its doors open to all who care to enter. It ministers down the years long after those who built it are gone. It is a gift from Today to Tomorrow.

CHURCHES WORTH SEEING

(NOTE: In this listing we have consciously avoided churches which are out of the moderate-price category, on the theory that such buildings would have features not available to the "average" building congregation.)

LARGE CHURCHES FOLLOWING NEW PATTERNS

Christian Church, Columbus, Indiana
Christ Lutheran Church, Minneapolis, Minnesota
First Baptist Church, Flint, Michigan

These are examples of the work of Eliel Saarinen. They are notable for their conscious lack of symmetry, unusual height, clean-cut lines, and the marked focusing of light in the chancel area.

Lutheran Church of the Good Shepherd, Minneapolis,
   Minnesota
Congregational Church, Waseca, Minnesota

Designed by Hills, Gilbertson and Hayes, these churches are also in the Saarinen tradition.

Zion Lutheran Church, Portland, Oregon
Central Lutheran Church, Portland, Oregon

These churches reflect the distinguishing features of the Saarinen structures; but in addition architect Pietro Belluschi has made effective use of wood and has managed the lighting in both chancel and nave with unusual skill.

The Community Church, New York City
The Congregational Church, Manhasset, New York

These impressive, well-handled buildings are the work of Magoon and Salo. Equally effective are the churches' starkly simple interiors.

SMALL CHURCHES FOLLOWING NEW PATTERNS

Presbyterian Church, Cottage Grove, Oregon

The genius of Pietro Belluschi, at work on a small scale and in an intimate manner, creates one of the most intelligently original churches in America.

Village Lutheran Church, Bronxville, New York

The need for economy led to a truly beautiful structure here. Second-hand brick has been used by Perry Duncan for both the exterior and the interior most successfully, with saw-toothed windows giving ever-varying effects on a rich texture.

St. Clement's Episcopal Church, Alexandria, Virginia

With no outside windows whatever, rich lighting effects have been achieved by architect Joseph Saunders. The altar is in the center with the congregation seated on either side.

First Congregational Church, Springfield, Missouri

Designed by Richard P. Stahl, this place of worship is in the form of a parabola, with a flat roof.

St. James Evangelical and Reformed Church, Dearborn, Michigan

An interesting example of indoor-outdoor harmony by Earl Pellerin.

Lebanon Lutheran Church, Bristol, Connecticut

Here we see what imaginative decoration can do to dignify a small church.

Methodist Church, Mayville, New York

This village church follows wholly new lines.

CAMPUS-STYLE CHURCHES

Oneonta Congregational Church, South Pasadena, California

A five-acre lot comfortably accommodates the several buildings of this church.

First Congregational Church, Fresno, California

The interesting variety of buildings here doesn't leave much of the lot!

Rock Spring Congregational Church, Arlington, Virginia

An excellent example of expandable facilities.

First Plymouth Congregational Church, Lincoln, Nebraska

Although the rooms are connected, the principle is that of a campus.

A Central Entrance Serving Several Areas

First Baptist Church, Flint, Michigan

From a rotunda-like entrance one goes to the church, offices, parlor, and chapel.

St. Peter and St. Paul United Church, Cincinnati, Ohio

This church is a turned-over Y. Straight ahead from the entrance is the place of worship; to the left, religious education; to the right, social activities.

Combination of Narthex and Parlor

First Congregational Church, Waukegan, Illinois

Hospitality and worship, side by side, still go their separate ways. From the street you enter a parlor which is separated from the church by curtained French windows and doors.

Edgebrook Community Church, Chicago, Illinois

The same result achieved with doors.

Faith United Church, Chicago, Illinois

Here separation is achieved only by distance. The lounge, complete with fireplace, is at the rear of the church.

First Congregational Church, DeKalb, Illinois

This congregation went one step further: it is impossible to enter the church proper without passing through a large parlor, with its picture window, fireplace, and kitchenette.

CHURCH SCHOOL FACILITIES

Trinity Evangelical and Reformed Church, St. Petersburg, Florida

A separate building for pre-school children.

Community Church, South Bend, Indiana

The educational unit here features a motel-like arrangement for classrooms.

Zion Evangelical and Reformed Church, Mount Clemens, Michigan

Outside walls of clear glass feature this wholly new pattern of large rooms which flow into one another. Several of the rooms look out on a patio garden.

Neighborhood Congregational Church, Pasadena, California

The children's rooms—again, glass-fronted—look out on both a garden and a playground.

First Congregational Church, Billings, Montana

This downtown church makes use of furniture to delineate the teaching areas in the delightful children's rooms.

Congregational Church, New Canaan, Connecticut

Wisely planned storage space; large rooms with continuous windows.

CHAPELS

Park Church, Grand Rapids, Michigan

A wide variety of functions can be accommodated in this easily accessible place of worship.

St. Peter and St. Paul United Church, Cincinnati, Ohio

The emphasis is on intimacy both in the size and the elaboration of the decorations.

First Congregational Church, Long Beach, California

Effectively designed with an eye for weddings.

PARKING LOTS

Congregational Church, Manhasset, New York

Room for 275 cars with methods of handling well worked out.

Federated Church, Richfield, Ohio

This church wisely turns its back to the highway and has its entrances entirely from an ample parking lot.

Oneonta Congregational Church, South Pasadena, California

Here the parking lot serves as the physical center, with the buildings used by the church arranged around it.

LIGHTING

Church of the Manger, Bethlehem, Pennsylvania

A small church bathed in daylight.

Community Church, Bellevue, Washington

Saw-toothed walls direct the light forward. Parabolic arches support the roof.

Church of the Heavenly Rest, New York City

The nave is lighted wholly from the rear wall.

First Congregational Church, Moline, Illinois

By placing the chancel lights on a rood beam, many interesting effects are achieved.

St. George's Episcopal Church, New York City

Without discarding the old pattern of hanging lanterns, new and brilliant results have been obtained.

Chester Hill Methodist Church, Mount Vernon, New York

An illustration of strong down-lighting from the ceiling of a high church.

CROSS AS AN EFFECTIVE EXTERNAL SYMBOL

Episcopal Church, Menlo Park, California

This cross has a background of plaster which can be illuminated at night and seen from one of the main highways of the Pacific Coast.

Congregational Church, Euclid, Ohio

A stark cross, somewhat relieved by greenery, dominates the church.

Trinity Lutheran Church, La Crosse, Wisconsin

Much roof, little side wall, tremendous cross.

Lakeside Presbyterian Church, San Francisco, California

Glass bricks are used to form a cross in the wall above the communion table—again with high visibility from a busy thoroughfare.

The Church in Silver Lake, Cuyahoga Falls, Ohio

A dark wooden cross is suspended against a white wooden wall on the side of the church next to the highway.

AIR CONDITIONING—IN THE NORTH

First Congregational Church, Springfield, Missouri

Achieved economically in this small church.

Third Baptist Church, St. Louis, Missouri

A complete job on a large building.

First Methodist Church, Chicago, Illinois

A welcome respite from the big city's heat.

RADIANT HEAT

Community Church, Glenview, Illinois

Comfortable on the coldest day in winter.

Village Lutheran Church, Bronxville, New York

Satisfactory on the whole, but there is something of a problem when the outside temperature rises suddenly.

INSULATION

Trinity Evangelical and Reformed Church, Deer Park, Cincinnati, Ohio

Effective sound insulation between the upper and lower floors on a side hill site.

UNUSUAL USE OF GLASS

First Bethany Evangelical and Reformed Church, Detroit, Michigan

Glass brick in the wall forms a cross which shines through the dossal; an interesting social and church school arrangement.

Episcopal Chapel, University of Connecticut, Storrs, Connecticut

A glass roof lets in much daylight, but at a sufficient height to be unobjectionable.

Evangelical United Brethren Church, Owosso, Michigan

Remarkable use of glass and greenery around the spacious entrance.

Wesley Methodist Church, Elgin, Illinois

One side entirely of glass; excellent use of side hill site.

Faith-Salem Evangelical and Reformed Church, St. Louis, Missouri

One wall of glass has been glorified in a most original way by Emil Frei.

St. Barnabas Episcopal Church, Ardsley, New York

A rugged profile with the entrance end entirely of glass.

Community Church, Alpine, California (near San Diego)

Striking reredos panels of vitreous enamel on copper.

Peace Evangelical and Reformed Church, Rochester, Minnesota

A simple building, this church is rich in symbols.

St. John's Episcopal Church, Midland, Michigan

Cloisters, clerestory, free-standing altar.

Our Saviour's Lutheran Church, Hibbing, Minnesota

A large carving of Christ on the cross against a brick wall is illuminated by natural light from one side.

St. John's Lutheran Church, Midland, Michigan

A "church in the round" with altar in the center, seven "sides" of pews, with an eighth section given over to the pulpit and choir.

Congregational Church, Grinnell, Iowa

A library off the narthex; organ and choir in rear balcony.

DISTINCTIVE EXTERIORS

Falcon Heights Congregational Church, St. Paul, Minnesota

A "ship" church with small side windows of excellent stained glass.

All Souls' Parish House Church, Bangor, Maine.

A modern wing on a French Gothic church which fits surprisingly well, with fascinating views from large windows.

St. Elizabeth's Church, Burien, Washington

Made unique by curving roof and curving walls. The most revolutionary church on the list!